Living
Faiths

Judaism
Teacher Guide

Sue Schraer
Series Editor: Janet Dyson
Consultant: Robert Bowie

OXFORD
UNIVERSITY PRESS

Contents

Scheme of Work

This table shows links to themes in RE across the six faiths in the *Living Faiths* series, so that you can easily navigate through the series and teach by religion or by theme. The themes are organized alphabetically under the two headings, **Beliefs** and **Moral and Ethical Issues**.

	Buddhism	Christianity	Hinduism	Islam	Judaism	Sikhism
Beliefs						
Faith origins	Overview, 1.1	Overview	Overview, 2.1	Overview	Overview	Overview
Festivals / Celebrations	2.5, 2.6	3.5, 5.2	3.2, 3.3		2.6, 3.4, 3.5, 3.7	2.6, 3.4, 3.5
Food	5.4		4.4, 4.5	3.3, 3.5	3.2	3.6, 3.7
God / Divine		1.1, 1.2, 1.3, 1.4	1.1, 1.2, 4.6	1.2	1.1, 1.3	1.1, 1.2
Key teachings	1.3, 1.4, 2.3, 2.4, 3.5	1.3, 1.6, 2.2, 4.4, 4.7	1.3, 1.4, 1.6, 3.1, 3.4, 3.5, 4.1	1.1, 1.3, 1.5, 3.1, 3.2, 3.3, 3.4	1.2, 1.4, 1.5, 2.2, 2.5	1.3, 1.4
Life after death	1.6, 2.6	2.5, 2.6	1.3	4.1, 4.2	4.2, 4.3	1.4
Places of worship	2.7	2.5, 3.2	2.5	2.5, 3.4	3.3	3.3
Religious leaders	4.3, 5.5, 5.6	2.3	1.5, 2.4, 2.5, 3.1, 4.2	2.2, 2.3	1.5, 2.7	2.1, 2.2, 2.3, 2.4
Religious symbols / Dress	1.5, 3.3	3.1	2.1	3.6	3.6	3.1, 3.2
Sacred texts	2.1, 2.2	2.1, 2.2	2.2, 2.3	2.1, 2.4	2.1, 2.2, 2.3, 2.4	2.5
Worship	3.1, 3.2, 3.3, 3.4	1.5, 2.4, 3.2, 3.3, 3.4	3.2, 3.4, 3.6	1.3, 1.5, 3.1, 3.2, 3.3, 3.4	3.1, 3.3	3.3
Moral and Ethical Issues						
Environment / Animal rights	5.4	5.4	4.4, 4.6, 4.7	4.5	4.6	4.2
Evil and suffering	1.3, 1.4	4.3, 4.5	4.2, 4.3	4.3, 4.4	4.5	5.2
Fair trade	4.4	5.5	5.5			
Gender and equality / Role of women	5.2		1.5, 5.4	3.6, 5.2	5.3	5.4
Interfaith	4.3	5.6	5.6	2.2, 5.6	5.5	5.6
Medical ethics	3.6	4.2	4.2	5.4	4.1	4.4, 4.5
Relationships / Marriage / Family	5.2	5.2, 5.3	3.3, 5.3	5.2, 5.3	5.1, 5.2	4.6
Science and religion	4.5	4.1		4.6, 5.4		4.3
Secular and atheist worldviews	4.5		1.1, 1.6	5.5	4.4, 5.5	4.3
War and peace	4.2, 5.5, 5.6	4.5, 4.6	3.1, 4.2, 5.5	4.3	5.5	5.2, 5.5
Wealth / Poverty / Charity	5.3	5.1, 5.6	3.1, 5.1	3.2	5.4	3.6, 3.8, 4.1

How we live now

Living Faiths draws on the rich heritage of culture and diversity in twenty-first century Britain. The series focuses on case studies (shown through film and print) of young people and their families in the UK who describe how their faith affects the way they live and the moral and ethical decisions they make. The emphasis is on the personal significance of religious faith, exploring the question: What does it *mean* to be a Buddhist, Christian, Hindu, Jew, Muslim or Sikh?

This approach allows students to experience the subject fully and see its relevance to their own lives. Engagement with the case study families creates awareness of diversity, encouraging respect and enhancing social awareness. Hearing and seeing young people sharing their faith and aspects of their daily lives helps students clarify their own perspectives and reflect on their experiences, build their sense of identity and belonging, challenge prejudices and provide the knowledge and understanding to enable them to flourish in their communities.

Flexible and adaptable

Living Faiths is a series of six books, teacher guides and online resources covering Buddhism, Christianity, Hinduism, Islam, Judaism, and Sikhism. The series is designed to allow teachers the flexibility to teach by faiths or by themes, and the Scheme of Work (on page 3) provides guidance at a glance on how to teach by themes. Through structured questioning and activities, students are encouraged to make links as they learn about a range of faiths and secular world views. They are expected to identify similarities and differences within faiths, and the *Teacher Guide* further provides suggestions on how to compare and contrast between faiths. There is a strong emphasis on sources including sacred texts, film interviews, audio and music

to give students access to the lived experience of the case study families and learn what their faith means in practice.

Pedagogy

The series takes a mixed pedagogical approach inspired by the important ethnographic work that has been developed in RE in recent years. Throughout the series students are introduced to the study of faith as it is practised by believers today. The enquiry-driven focus enables them to engage with the voices and personalities of faith, getting beyond generalizations and over-simplifications, to enter into dialogue with people about their faith. Through this dialogue with living faith, students will be encouraged to reflect on the experiences and beliefs of others and also on their own experiences of faith, belief and what really matters in life.

The *Living Faiths* series has been designed to engage, interest and challenge students. Each unit has an intriguing title, often a question, to capture the interest of students as soon as the lesson begins. The 'starter' activities get students thinking and discussing, drawing on their prior learning or their personal experiences as ways into the main lesson focus.

Questioning

Questioning is fundamental to good teaching and learning. Higher order questions enable students to tackle issues at a deep level and extend their thinking, develop independence in the way they learn and think and come to a fuller understanding of an idea because they have tried to explain it themselves. Bloom's Taxonomy (1956), is a useful tool for planning sequences of different types of questions of increasing difficulty to promote higher order thinking. Many of the activities are designed for pair and group discussion or for independent and small group research to promote student participation. Through the activities, students will develop the ability to speculate, to raise their own questions and seek answers for themselves.

Reflection

Reflection

How and why might a place be significant to a faith? Do you have a special place? Why is it special?

ctivities

Before the Israelites arrived, the land of Canaan already had a number of tribal groups living there in small, fortified settlements. What problems do you think the arrival of the Jews might have caused?

What challenges did the Jewish people face in keeping their faith in a promise that might not come true for a long time? Write two short diary entries.

a One from the point of view of a Jew with a very strong faith in the purpose of God.

b One from the point of view of a Jew who has doubts.

❸ 'Everyone should have a dream for the future, even if it seems an impossible dream.' Do you agree or disagree with this statement? Give your reasons.

The activities are colour coded to identify three modes of thinking that are particularly valuable in the study of religion, philosophy and the broad area of social sciences.

Students are encouraged to:
- **Red: 'Think like a theologian'** these questions focus on understanding the nature of religious belief, its symbolism and spiritual significance; in the *Student Book* they are highlighted by a red question number
- **Blue: 'Think like a philosopher'** these questions focus on analysing and debating big ideas such as truth and reality; in the *Student Book* they are highlighted by a blue question number
- **Green: 'Think like a social scientist'** these questions focus on exploring and analysing why people do what they do and how belief affects action; in the *Student Book* they are highlighted by a green question number

Reflection

Reflection helps students to deepen their thinking and apply their learning about the religious beliefs and practices of others. It encourages them to explore their own beliefs in the light of what they learn, whether they are religious or not, and how they impact on personal ethics.

Thinking skills

In RE, students are expected to think in increasing depth about complex issues to do with faith, beliefs, ideas and motivation. Philosophical enquiry-based approaches such as mind-mapping help students to think creatively, analytically and critically; to listen to, evaluate and respond to the views and ideas of others; to give reasons for their opinions, make connections and hypothesize; to give both sides of an argument, evaluate and draw conclusions.

Assessment

At the end of each unit there is a final assessment task which draws together students' learning.

Assessment for learning strategies are built into every unit:
- Learning objectives for each unit are written in student-friendly language and shared with students
- Students know what standards and levels they are aiming for
- Self- and peer-assessment opportunities are supported by 'I can' statements
- **AT1 Learning *about* religion** is assessed using auto-marked tests to help save you time setting questions and marking
- **AT2 Learning *from* religion** is assessed with step-by-step tasks and support materials. These use effective assessment for learning strategies to help students recognize next steps and improve performance.

We hope that you will enjoy using this series to bring real families of faith into the classroom, and to introduce students to the liveliness and relevance of religious education.

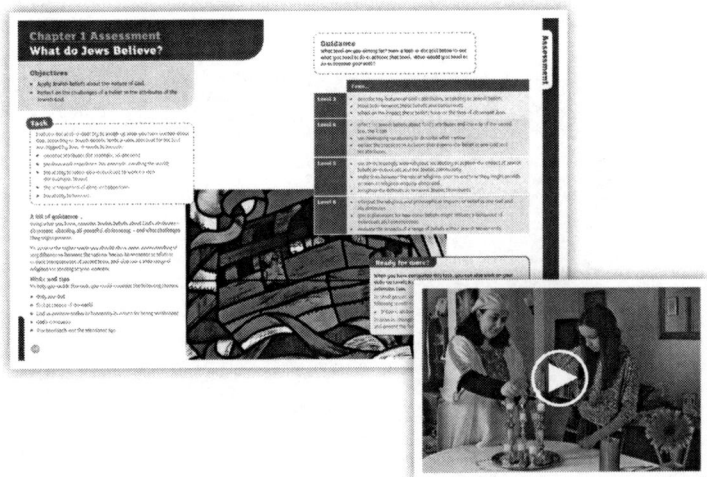

Janet Dyson
(Series Editor)

Robert Bowie
(Series Consultant)

5

About this Series

Living Faiths Judaism is one of six Religious Education Student Books covering the following major faiths: Buddhism, Christianity, Hinduism, Islam, Judaism, and Sikhism. This series fully integrates real-life film clips and other exciting multimedia resources on the *Oxbox Online* with the *Student Books* and *Teacher Guides*, so your lessons can be delivered easily and seamlessly.

The series components

The series consist of:

For students

- Six *Student Books* (and/or six *Online Student Books*)
- Six *OxBox Online* Lessons, Resources and Assessments.

For teachers

- Six *Teacher Guides*
- Six *OxBox Online* Lessons, Resources and Assessments (includes teacher access to the accompanying *Online Student Book*).

Student Book

The *Living Faiths Judaism Student Book* uses **real-life case studies** to encourage students to ask questions, actively engage with **moral** and **ethical** issues, and reflect on the relevance of RE.

> Starter activities spark your students' interest in new topics

> The 'Reflection' feature helps your students to consider beliefs and practices of others, and how they link to their own lives and beliefs

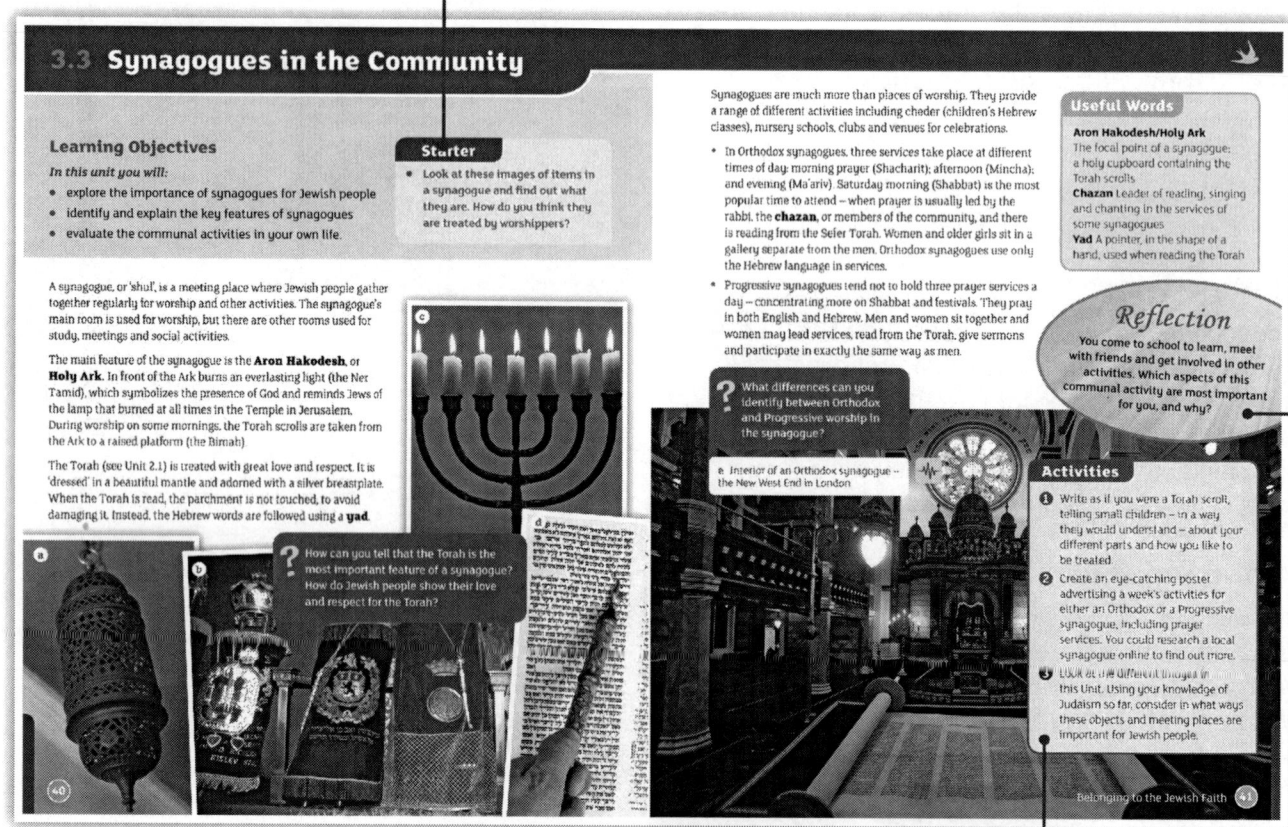

Judaism Student Book

> Colour-coded activities develop varied skills and are structured to encourage progression and allow differentiation

Case studies provide first-hand experience of real Jewish families talking about their faith

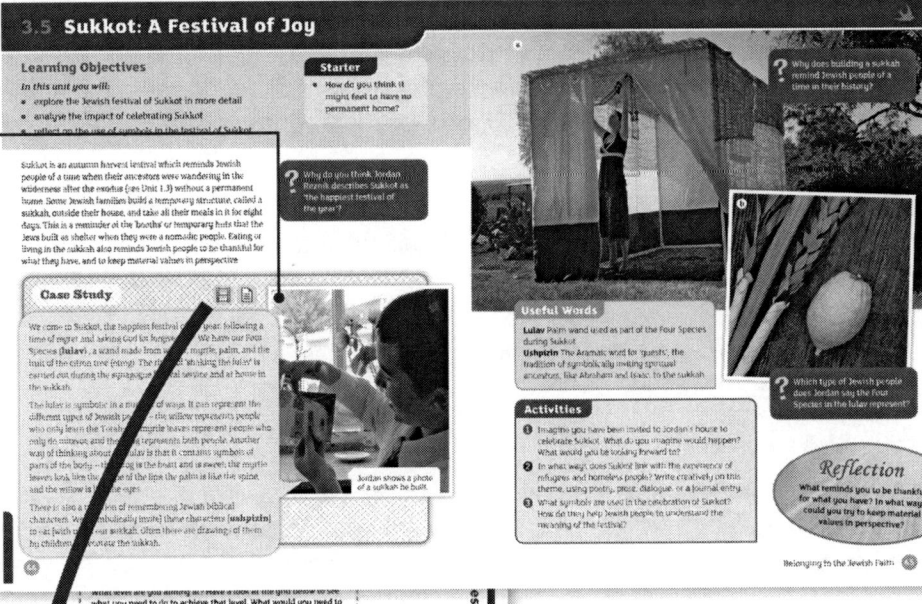

3.5 Sukkot: A Festival of Joy

Learning Objectives

In this unit you will:
- explore the Jewish festival of Sukkot in more detail
- analyse the impact of celebrating Sukkot
- reflect on the use of symbols in the festival of Sukkot

Starter
- How do you think it might feel to have no permanent home?

Sukkot is an autumn harvest festival which reminds Jewish people of a time when their ancestors were wandering in the wilderness after the exodus (see Unit 1.3) without a permanent home. Some Jewish families build a temporary structure, called a sukkah, outside their house, and take all their meals in it for eight days. This is a reminder of the 'booths' or temporary huts that the Jews built as shelter when they were a nomadic people. Eating or living in the sukkah also reminds Jewish people to be thankful for what they have, and to keep material values in perspective.

Why do you think Jordan Reznik describes Sukkot as 'the happiest festival of the year'?

Why does building a sukkah remind Jewish people of a time in their history?

Case Study

We come to Sukkot, the happiest festival of the year, following a time of regret and asking God for forgiveness. We hand our Four Species (lulav), a wand made from willow, myrtle, palm, and the fruit of the citron tree (etrog). The ritual of waving the lulav is carried out during the synagogue morning service and at home in the sukkah.

The lulav is symbolic in a number of ways. It can represent the different types of Jewish people – the willow represents people who only learn the Torah, the myrtle leaves represent people who only do mitzvot, and the etrog represents both people. Another way of thinking about the lulav is that it contains symbols of parts of the body – the etrog is the heart and is sweet, the myrtle leaves look like the shape of the lips, the palm is like the spine, and the willow is like the eyes.

There is also a tradition of remembering Jewish biblical characters. We symbolically invite these characters (ushpizin) to eat with us in the sukkah. Often there are drawings of them by children to decorate the sukkah.

Jordan shows a photo of a sukkah he built.

Useful Words

Lulav Palm wand used as part of the Four Species during Sukkot
Ushpizin The Aramaic word for 'guests', the tradition of symbolically inviting spiritual ancestors, like Abraham and Isaac, to the sukkah

Which type of Jewish people does Jordan say the Four Species in the lulav represent?

Activities
1. Imagine you have been invited to Jordan's house to celebrate Sukkot. What do you imagine would happen? What would you be looking forward to?
2. In what ways does Sukkot link with the experience of refugees and homeless people? Write creatively on this theme, using poetry, prose, dialogue, or a journal entry.
3. What symbols are used in the celebration of Sukkot? How do they help Jewish people to understand the meaning of the festival?

Reflection
What reminds you to be thankful for what you have? In what ways could you try to keep material values in perspective?

Belonging to the Jewish Faith

Judaism Student Book

Chapter 3 Assessment
Belonging to the Jewish Faith

Objectives
- Consider how Jewish people live day-to-day.
- Apply your knowledge about Judaism reflectively.
- Analyse the diversity in religious expression across the range of Jewish Movements.

Task
Choose three of the most significant facts that you have discovered about living day-to-day as a Jew. Write a magazine article explaining these for a target audience of young people who know nothing at all about Judaism. Write in a lively and interesting style.

A bit of guidance...
Explain any Hebrew or useful words in brackets as you go along.

To achieve the higher levels, you should show some understanding of any differences between the various Jewish movements in relation to your chosen themes, and also use a wide range of religious vocabulary in your answers.

Hints and tips:
To help you tackle this task, you could consider some of the following themes:
- Dietary laws
- Shabbat observance
- Festivals
- Religious dress and what it means
- How life stages are marked
- Sacred texts

What level are you aiming at? Have a look at the grid below to see what you need to do to achieve that level. What would you need to do to improve your work?

	I can...
Level 3	• describe some key features of Judaism • ask questions about what is involved in belonging to the Jewish faith • reflect on my own responses to answers
Level 4	• show understanding of what it means to belong to the Jewish faith • explain how belonging to the Jewish faith impacts daily life • support answers with evidence
Level 5	• explain, using a wide range of religious vocabulary, the impact of belonging to the Jewish faith on individuals and communities • make relevant links to my own life and experiences • ask questions and suggest answers about different interpretations of sacred texts which impact on how Jewish people express their Judaism
Level 6	• use religious and philosophical language to evaluate the practice of Judaism • analyse the effect of different movements within the Jewish faith, and how they express their sense of belonging • analyse, using arguments and examples, how belonging to a faith group, such as Judaism, impacts on people's sense of history and identity

Ready for more?
When you have completed this task, you can also work on your skills for Levels 6 and 7, and perhaps even higher. This is an extension task.

Choose a theme from the hints and tips section that you did not write about in your article.
- Prepare a speech that includes a PowerPoint presentation aimed at conveying information and stimulating discussion. You could also include artefacts or outside speakers. Be inventive!
- Create a practical exercise which will help the audience to understand the topic.
- Give examples of the differences between Jewish Movements.

There is an assessment spread for every chapter in the *Student Book* to help students determine what level they are aiming for and make progress

Extensions tasks within assessments challenge more able students

Case studies are linked directly to films on the *OxBox Online* and are marked with film icons on each page

Judaism OxBox Online

Authors

Experienced RE Consultant **Janet Dyson** and well-known author and PGCE tutor **Robert Bowie** lead the author **Sue Schraer**, who is an experienced teacher.

Using this Book

 ## Teacher Guide

The *Living Faiths Judaism Teacher Guide* aims to save you time and effort. It provides **full support** and guidance for the *Judaism Student Book*, including **practical tasks** and **creative suggestions** for incorporating differentiation into your teaching.

What it provides

For each chapter of the student book, this book provides:

- a chapter overview
- help at a glance for each unit
- further suggestions for class and homework
- an assessment overview.

It also has a **Glossary** at the back, covering the RE terms students will meet.

Please turn to the **Contents List** on page 2 to see how this book is structured. While the Living Faiths series is organized by religion, a **Scheme of Work** on page 3 is also provided to help you teach RE **by themes**.

Find out more about the four main components below.

The chapter overview

This is your introduction to the corresponding *Student Book* chapter.

Shows how the *Student Book* chapter relates to the KS3 RE Programme of Study (non-statutory)

Reminds you that some lessons, including starters and plenaries, will need resources prepared in advance

Sets out the key ideas within, and behind, the chapter in the *Student Book*

Chapter 1 Overview
What do Jews Believe?

Points you to the assessment material for the chapter (summative and formal assessments, and related resources)

Gives a brief summary of what's covered in the *Student Book* chapter. It will help you give students a road-map for the chapter

Sets out the objectives and outcomes for the chapter, and the corresponding unit numbers

Help at a glance for each unit

These pages give comprehensive help for each unit of the *Student Book*.

Summarizes ideas covered in the unit, plus underlying ideas where appropriate

Starts with a brief walk through the unit, to show you how it develops

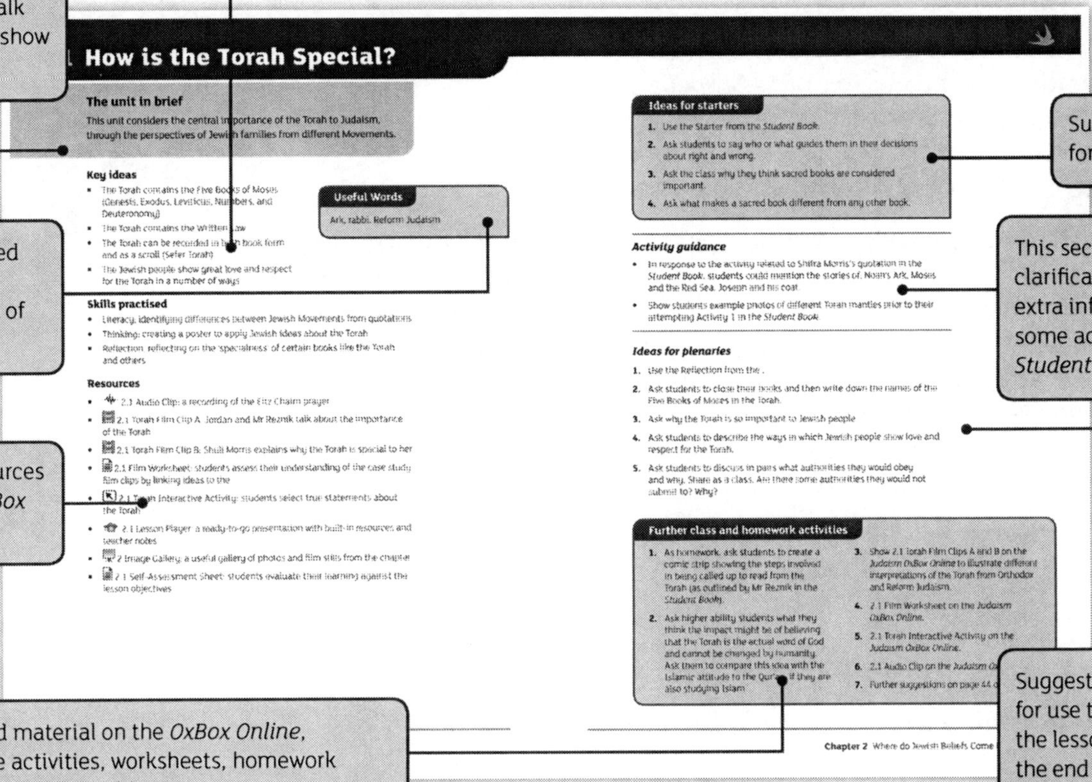

New terms introduced in the unit. See the glossary at the back of the book

A list of all the resources available on the *OxBox Online* for the unit

Points you to related material on the *OxBox Online*, including interactive activities, worksheets, homework ideas and assessment opportunities

Suggestions for starters

This section provides clarification and extra information for some activities in the *Student Book*

Suggests plenaries for use throughout the lesson, not just at the end

How is the Torah Special?

The unit in brief

This unit considers the central importance of the Torah to Judaism, through the perspectives of Jewish families from different Movements.

Key ideas
- The Torah contains the Five Books of Moses (Genesis, Exodus, Leviticus, Numbers, and Deuteronomy)
- The Torah contains the Written Law
- The Torah can be recorded in book form and as a scroll (Sefer Torah)
- The Jewish people show great love and respect for the Torah in a number of ways

Useful Words

Ark, rabbi, Reform Judaism

Skills practised
- Literacy: identifying differences between Jewish Movements from quotations
- Thinking: creating a poster to apply Jewish ideas about the Torah
- Reflection: reflecting on the specialness of certain books like the Torah and others

Resources
- 2.1 Audio Clip: a recording of the Eitz Chaim prayer
- 2.1 Torah Film Clip A: Jordan and Mr Reznik talk about the importance of the Torah
- 2.1 Torah Film Clip B: Shuli Morris explains why the Torah is special to her
- 2.1 Film Worksheet: students assess their understanding of the case study film clips by linking ideas to the
- 2.1 Torah Interactive Activity: students select true statements about the Torah
- 2.1 Lesson Player: a ready-to-go presentation with built-in resources and teacher notes
- 2 Image Gallery: a useful gallery of photos and film stills from the chapter
- 2.1 Self-Assessment Sheet: students evaluate their learning against the lesson objectives

Ideas for starters
1. Use the Starter from the *Student Book*.
2. Ask students to say who or what guides them in their decisions about right and wrong.
3. Ask the class why they think sacred books are considered important.
4. Ask what makes a sacred book different from any other book.

Activity guidance
- In response to the activity related to Shira Morris's quotation in the *Student Book*, students could mention the stories of Noah's Ark, Moses and the Red Sea, Joseph and his coat.
- Show students example photos of different Torah mantles prior to their attempting Activity 1 in the *Student Book*.

Ideas for plenaries
1. Use the Reflection from the .
2. Ask students to close their books and then write down the names of the Five Books of Moses in the Torah.
3. Ask why the Torah is so important to Jewish people.
4. Ask students to describe the ways in which Jewish people show love and respect for the Torah.
5. Ask students to discuss in pairs what authorities they would obey and why. Share as a class. Are there some authorities they would not submit to? Why?

Further class and homework activities
1. As homework, ask students to create a comic strip showing the steps involved in being called up to read from the Torah (as outlined by Mr Reznik in the *Student Book*).
2. Ask higher ability students what they think the impact might be of believing that the Torah is the actual word of God and cannot be changed by humanity. Ask them to compare this idea with the Islamic attitude to the Qur'an if they are also studying Islam.
3. Show 2.1 Torah Film Clips A and B on the Judaism OxBox Online to illustrate different interpretations of the Torah from Orthodox and Reform Judaism.
4. 2.1 Film Worksheet on the Judaism OxBox Online.
5. 2.1 Torah Interactive Activity on the Judaism OxBox Online.
6. 2.1 Audio Clip on the Judaism O
7. Further suggestions on page 44

Chapter 2 Where do Jewish Beliefs Come

Further suggestions for class and homework

These pages give a bank of further suggestions for class and homework.

They have been graded *, ** or *** according to level of difficulty.

These suggestions are addressed directly to students.

1.1 There is Only One God
1. Write a letter to a rabbi asking him everything that puzzles you about God. *
2. Devise a role-play between a believer and a non-believer in one God. **
3. Design a logo for clothing which reminds the

2. Role-play a dispute about a contract. *
3. In a small group, devise a contract (e.g. about Behaviour at Lunch time). What might be a sign to seal the deal? *
4. How might the nature of God be revealed through the covenants with Adam and Noah? ***
5. Look at the Ten Commandments in Exodus 20.

Suggestions are graded, but some are suitable for all levels, and differentiated by outcome

The assessment overview

This section introduces you to the end-of-chapter assessment task from the *Student Book*, and describes the support materials available for the chapter.

The purpose of the end-of-chapter assessment task from the *Student Book* is summarized

Assessment in the *Student Book*

You will find an assessment task at the end of every chapter which focuses on AT2. In this chapter, the task asks students to write a work appraisal for the God worshipped by the Jews.

In the *Student Book* (and on the supporting worksheets), you'll find guidance about levels of assessment that you can use to help your students understand what their work should include. You could ask them to use these criteria for self- or peer-assessment once they've completed the task.

Living Faiths Assessment

Student Book
- Assessment Task
- Levels Guidance

OxBox Online
- Auto-Marked Test
- Assessment Task Presentation
- Assessment Worksheets

You can see all the assessment materials available for the chapter at a glance

OxBox Online

Living Faiths Judaism OxBox Online is packed full of guided support and ideas for running and creating effective lessons on Judaism. It's intuitive to use, customizable, and can be accessed online.

It consists of:

- Judaism Lessons, Resources and Assessments (includes teacher access to the accompanying *Online Student Book*)
- *Judaism Online Student Book*.

Lessons, Resources and Assessment

Living Faiths Judaism OxBox Online – Lessons, Resources and Assessment provides over one hundred lively built-in resources, including unique specially commissioned films of real Jewish families practising their faiths, interactive activities, ready-to-go lesson presentations, and supported assessment tasks. You can even **adapt** many of these resources to suit you and your students' individual needs, and **upload** your existing resources so everything can be accessed from one location. Image collections and audio clips are also included to help bring RE to life in your classroom.

Lessons, Resources and Assessment provides:

- Resources
- Lessons
- Assessment and Markbook
- Teacher access to the *Online Student Book*.

Find out more about the four main components below.

Resources

Click on the **Resources tab** at the top of the screen to access the full list of *Living Faiths Judaism* resources.

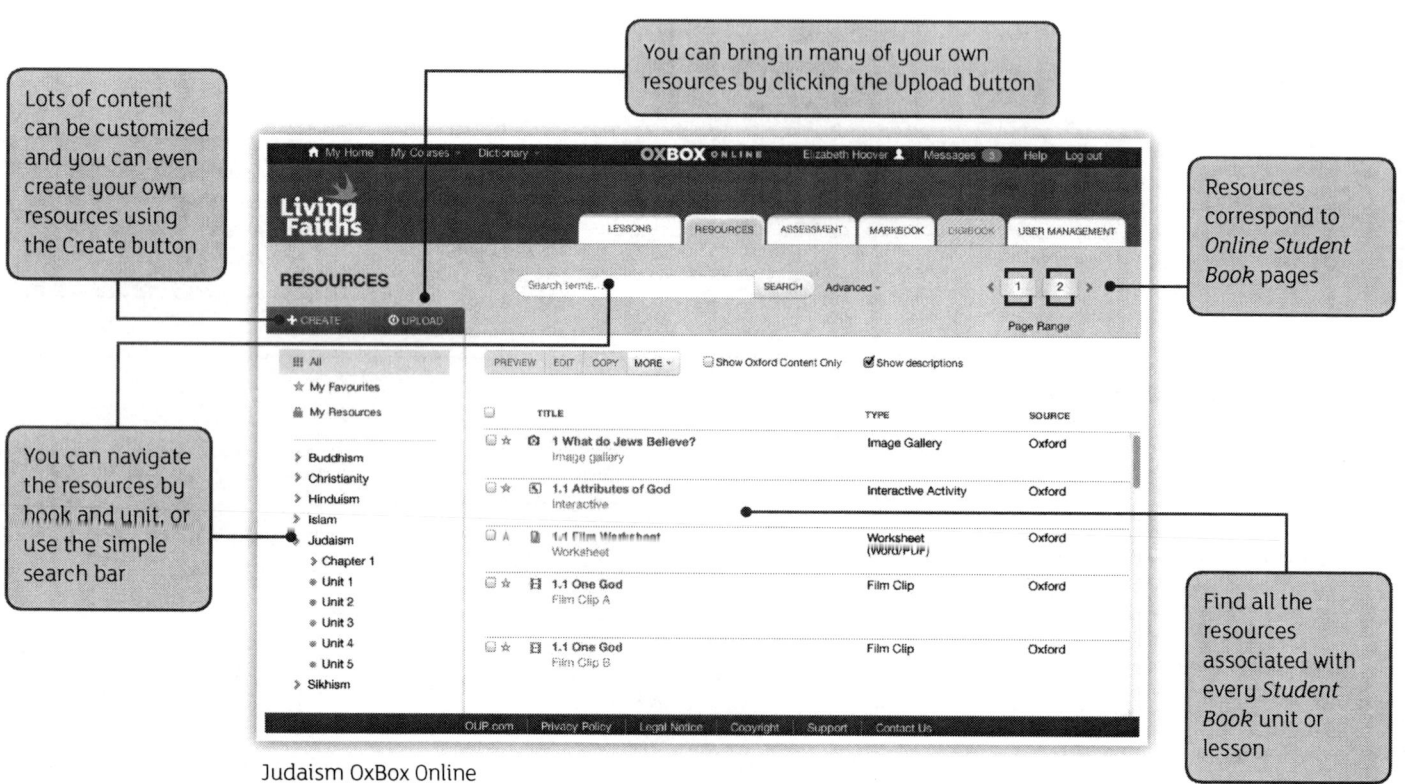

Judaism OxBox Online

The Resources section has more than:

 20 Film clips: Specially commissioned films help your students to engage actively with RE through watching real Jewish families practise their faith and to explore the diversity within Judaism.

 10 Audio clips: Specially commissioned music and narrated sources help bring RE alive in your classroom.

 70 Worksheets: Creative worksheets that help provide differentiation/extension material for each unit, and film worksheets to help students assess their own learning of the case study film clips and link ideas back to the *Student Book* unit. They are provided as PDFs, which you can print off and photocopy, and as Word files, which you can amend to suit your students' needs.

 30 Interactive activities: Various types of activities are available for each unit as short main activities, plenaries or summative assessments. They can also be used for independent study. Most of these activities are auto-marked to help you save time marking.

 80 Images: An image gallery with captions is provided for each chapter so you can easily enlarge any photo or artwork from the *Student Book* on screen and use it as a discussion starter, use them in your own worksheets, or give them to students to use in class or homework activities.

OxBox Online Resources are fully integrated with the *Student Book*:

Judaism
Student Book

Real Jewish families are featured in the *Student Book* and you can find the specially commissioned films related to *Student Book* units on *OxBox Online*

Use the accompanying film worksheets to help your students consolidate what they have learnt

All the resources and assessments are **fully integrated** with the *Judaism Student Book*

OxBox Online

Lesson presentations

Click on the **Lessons tab** to access the full list of *Living Faiths Judaism* lessons and notes.

Ready-to-play lesson presentations complement every unit in the book. Each lesson presentation is easy to launch, and features unit objectives; the related starters; worksheets; film and interactive resources; and closes with a plenary activity or reflection. You can further **personalize** the lessons by adding in your own resources and notes. Your lessons and notes can be accessed by your whole department, and they are a great time-saver and **ideal for non-specialist** teachers and cover-lessons.

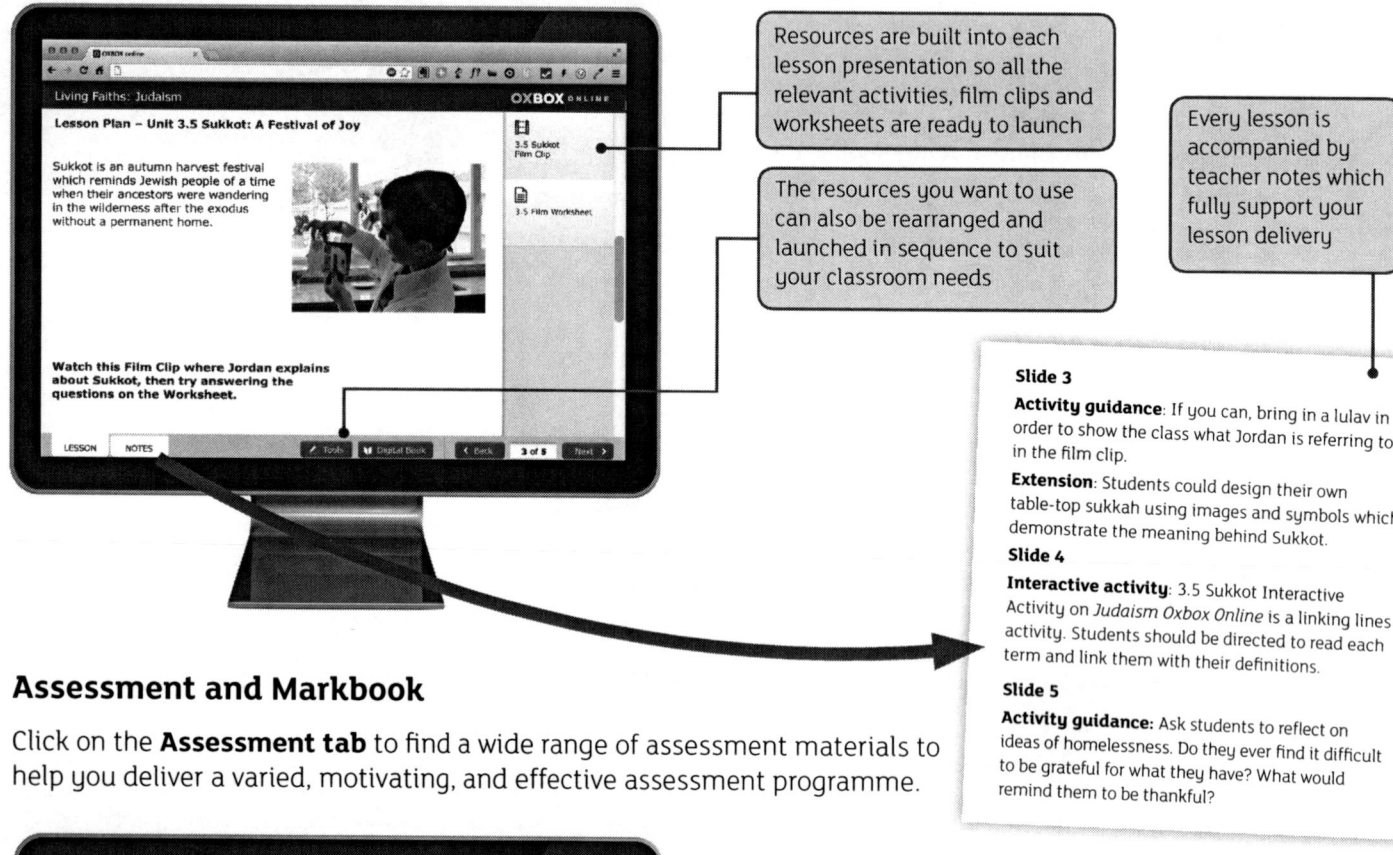

Resources are built into each lesson presentation so all the relevant activities, film clips and worksheets are ready to launch

The resources you want to use can also be rearranged and launched in sequence to suit your classroom needs

Every lesson is accompanied by teacher notes which fully support your lesson delivery

Slide 3

Activity guidance: If you can, bring in a lulav in order to show the class what Jordan is referring to in the film clip.

Extension: Students could design their own table-top sukkah using images and symbols which demonstrate the meaning behind Sukkot.

Slide 4

Interactive activity: 3.5 Sukkot Interactive Activity on *Judaism Oxbox Online* is a linking lines activity. Students should be directed to read each term and link them with their definitions.

Slide 5

Activity guidance: Ask students to reflect on ideas of homelessness. Do they ever find it difficult to be grateful for what they have? What would remind them to be thankful?

Assessment and Markbook

Click on the **Assessment tab** to find a wide range of assessment materials to help you deliver a varied, motivating, and effective assessment programme.

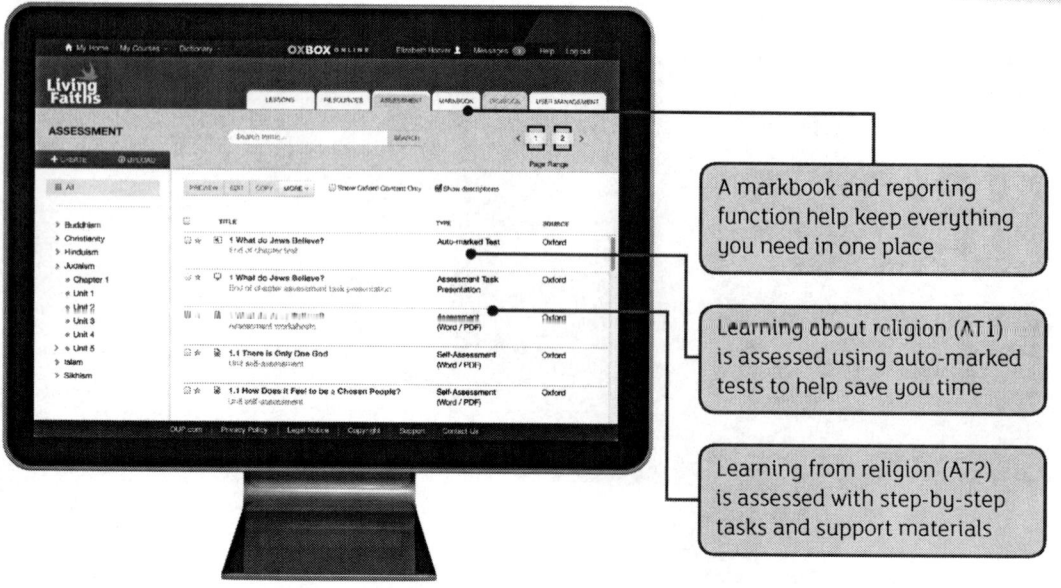

A markbook and reporting function help keep everything you need in one place

Learning about religion (AT1) is assessed using auto-marked tests to help save you time

Learning from religion (AT2) is assessed with step-by-step tasks and support materials

The Assessment section provides:

- **2 baseline tests:** These tests cover both **Attainment Target 1** (learning *about* religion) and **Attainment Target 2** (learning *from* religion), and they can help you to assess quickly the prior RE knowledge that your new KS3 students may have.

- **5 auto-marked tests**: Each end-of-chapter auto-marked test assesses **AT1**. The marks are automatically reported in the **Markbook tab**.

- **30 self-assessment worksheets**: Self-assessment worksheets help students to self- or peer-evaluate the skills they have learnt from each unit.

- **5 assessment task presentations**: Each end-of-chapter assessment task in the *Student Book*, which assesses **AT2**, has a front-of-class presentation for you to use to help guide students towards understanding and analysing what the question/task is asking of them. You can lead students through this step-by-step presentation and help them decide how to prepare to answer the question.

- **15 assessment worksheets**: These worksheets complement the assessment tasks in the *Student Book* and the assessment task presentations. They recap the task; provide a self-evaluation chart; and space for students to prepare their work.

A **Markbook** with reporting function completes the *OxBox Online* assessment package, so you can keep track of all your students' test results and assessment scores. This includes both the automarked tests and work that need to be marked by you. It is also easy to import class registers and create user accounts for all your students.

Online Student Book

The *Judaism Online Student Book* provides you with an on-screen version of the *Student Book* for you to use on your whiteboard with the whole class.

Teacher access to the *Online Student Book* is **automatically available** as part of the Lessons, Resources and Assessment package. You can also choose to buy access for your students.

Both teacher and student access include a simple bank of tools so you can personalize the book and take notes.

It can be accessed on other devices, such as tablets.

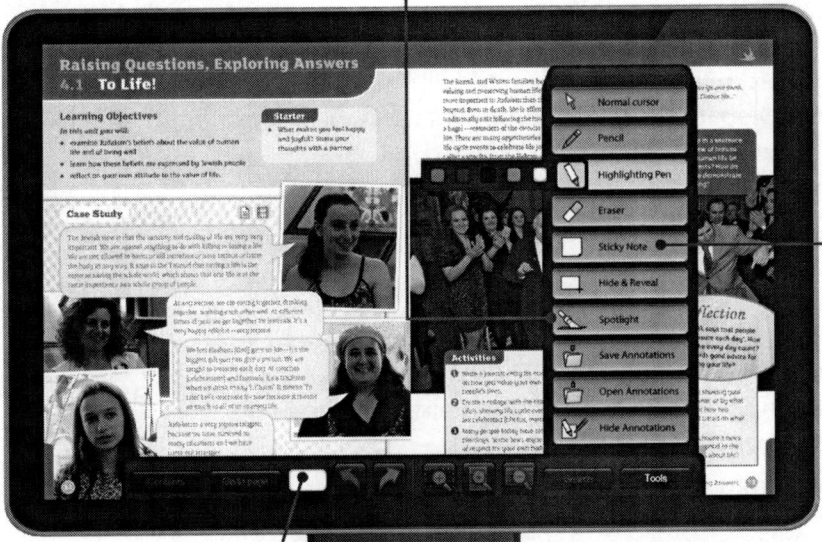

Zoom in and spotlight any part of the text

Use different tools such as Sticky Notes, Bookmarks and Pencil features to personalize each page

Navigate around the book quickly with the contents menu, keyword search or page number search

Every teacher and student has their own digital notebook for use within their *Online Student Book*. You can even choose to share some of your notes with your students, or hide them from view – all student notes are accessible to themselves only

Chapter 1 Overview
What do Jews Believe?

Helping you deliver Key Stage 3 RE

This chapter addresses the following areas of the Programme of Study:

Key concepts

Beliefs, teachings and sources
- Interpreting teachings, sources, authorities and ways of life in order to understand religions and beliefs
- Understanding and responding critically to beliefs and attitudes

Identity, diversity and belonging
- Understanding how individuals develop a sense of identity and belonging through faith or belief

Key processes

Learning about religion
- Investigate the impact of religious beliefs and teachings on individuals, communities and societies and the reasons for commitment
- Apply a wide range of religious and philosophical vocabulary consistently and accurately, recognizing both the power and limitations of language in expressing religious ideas and beliefs
- Analyse religious beliefs, arguments and ideas

Learning from religion
- Reflect on the relationship between beliefs, teachings, world issues and ultimate questions
- Evaluate beliefs, commitments and the impact of religion in the contemporary world

The big picture

These are the key ideas behind this chapter:

- A central belief in Judaism is that there is only one God who is all-powerful (omnipotent), all-knowing (omniscient), all-present (omnipresent) and all-loving (omnibenevolent).

- According to sacred texts, Jewish people are called by God to be a 'light to the nations'. Jewish people are 'chosen' by God to have a special relationship with Him, and be role-models for how humanity should live.

- Covenants are agreements made by God in return for humanity keeping the commandments. Adam, Noah, Abraham and Moses are examples of people who made important covenants with God in the Torah.

- God promised the Israelites (early Jewish people) the land of Canaan in return for their obedience. Many Jewish people were exiled from this land during the Roman Empire, and, for many Jewish people, returning to this land (now the modern State of Israel) remains a dream to this day.

- The purpose of keeping laws is to bring an age of peace to the world, either, as traditional Judaism believes, through a single leader (the Mashiach) or a human effort to repair the world (bringing about the Messianic Age).

Chapter outline

Use this to give students a mental road-map of the chapter:

1.1 There is Only One God – introduces the core Jewish belief in one God and God's attributes. A modern Orthodox Jewish family explain what they believe about God

1.2 How Does it Feel to be a Chosen People? – explains the concept of the Jewish people as chosen by God to be a 'light to the nations'

1.3 Covenants: Making a Deal With God – explores agreements made between God and humanity, including examples in Jewish sacred texts

1.4 A Land Flowing With Milk and Honey – introduces the idea that God promised the Jewish people a land in return for their obedience (explored in more detail in Unit 5.5)

1.5 A Better World: the Messianic Age – explores different Jewish views about the Mashiach and the Messianic Age, and what it means to try to create a better world

Opportunities for assessment

Baseline automarked test and assessment tasks are available on the *Judaism OxBox Online*. This allows you to evaluate how much knowledge students already have about Judaism before you start the course.

Summative assessments on the *Judaism OxBox Online* include automarked tests, interactive activities, and self-assessment worksheets.

The end-of-chapter assessment task in the *Student Book* provides formative assessment. Supporting materials for the assessment task can be found on the

Judaism OxBox Online, such as the Assessment Task Presentation and the related worksheets.

There are other opportunities for assessment too. For example, you could use some of the activities or reflection points throughout each *Student Book* unit, or some of the 'Further Suggestions' at the end of this chapter.

Getting ready for this chapter

- If you have the *Judaism OxBox Online*, watch the case study film clips in advance, so that you can prepare and guide students before and during their viewing.

- If possible, try to arrange for your students to visit a local synagogue, or invite a Jewish leader to come and share their core values.

Objectives and outcomes for this chapter

Objectives	Unit	Outcomes
Most students will:		Most students will be able to:
• analyse the impact on Jewish people of belief in one God • evaluate the Jewish belief in an invisible God • reflect on the impacts of belief in an all-loving God.	1.1	• Use key terms for belief in one God and explain how this belief influences Jewish people • explain the challenges to belief in an invisible God • identify evidence for and against God being all-loving.
• examine teachings from the Torah which describe the Jews as specially chosen by God • analyse the impact on Jews and non-Jews of the Jewish belief that they are a chosen people • reflect on whether they have a special reason for being in the world.	1.2	• give examples from the Torah indicating Jews as God's chosen people • explain some consequences of belief in Jews as God's chosen people for both Jews and non-Jews • identify possible roles and purposes for being in the world.
• explore the significance of the word 'covenant' to Jewish people • identify four key people who made covenants with God • reflect on the importance of signs to seal agreements.	1.3	• explain the meaning of covenant giving an example from the Torah • identify four key people and the covenants they are associated with • use key terms for signs of the covenants and explain their role and significance.
• examine the significance of the Promised Land to Jewish people • consider the particular importance of Jerusalem to Jewish people • reflect on the importance of special places to a faith and an individual.	1.4	• explain what is meant by the Promised Land and say why it might be important to Jewish people • state why Jerusalem is important to Jewish people • identify places that might be important to different faiths and say whether you have a special place.
• examine the Orthodox belief in a leader, or Mashiach (Messiah), bringing about a perfect world • consider what is needed to create a Messianic Age • reflect on the chances of ever achieving a perfect world.	1.5	• explain the concept of the Mashiach and identify the qualities Orthodox Jews believe the Mashiach will have • respond creatively to the idea of a Messianic Age • debate whether a perfect world is possible to achieve.

1.1 There is Only One God

The unit in brief

This unit focuses on the core Jewish belief in one God, as well as the nature of God as all-knowing, all-present, all-powerful and all-loving. Students meet a Modern Orthodox family and discover what they believe about God.

Key ideas

- Jewish people believe in only one God (monotheism)
- God is all-powerful, all-present, all-knowing, and all-loving
- God has no physical being

Skills practised

- Thinking: considering how it's possible to believe in something that's invisible
- Problem solving: analysing why the idea of more than one God might be illogical
- Reflection: considering the impact of belief in an all-loving God

Resources

- ∿ 1.1 Audio Clip: a recording of the Shema prayer
- 🎞 1.1 One God Film Clip A: The Reznik family talk about what they believe God is like
- 🎞 1.1 One God Film Clip B: Mr Reznik and Jordan talk about what they believe God is like
- 📄 1.1 Film Worksheet: students assess their understanding of the case study film clips by linking ideas to the *Student Book*
- ⬆ 1.1 Attributes of God Interactive Activity: students link key terms describing attributes of God with their definitions
- 🎓 1.1 Lesson Player: a ready-to-go presentation with built-in resources and teacher notes
- 🖥 1 Image Gallery: a useful gallery of photos and film stills from the chapter
- 📄 1.1 Self-Assessment Sheet: students evaluate their learning against the lesson objectives

Ideas for starters

1. Use the Starter from the *Student Book*.

2. Ask students whether they think God, or a 'spiritual' being, can be described. Divide the classroom into Yes and No zones, and ask them to vote accordingly. Ask some students to explain their decisions.

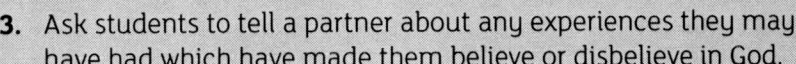

> **3.** Ask students to tell a partner about any experiences they may have had which have made them believe or disbelieve in God.

Activity guidance

For Activity 3 in the *Student Book,* you may wish to restrict students to either a visual or written format. If a visual format is used, you could use this as an opportunity to explain that Jewish people choose not to depict God visually.

Ideas for plenaries

1. Use the Reflection from the *Student Book*.

2. Ask students to write down all they can in two minutes about what Jewish people believe about God.

3. Ask students to discuss with a partner where Jewish beliefs about God come from.

4. Oscar Nominations! Ask students to write down the most interesting, most surprising and most difficult facts to understand from this unit. Feed back as a class.

5. Draw a blank mind-map or spider diagram on the board and ask students to call out four qualities that Jewish people believe God has.

6. University Challenge! Choose a panel of four and ask the other students to devise questions to ask them about the Jewish God.

7. Ask students to identify how it might feel to believe in a God who is invisible but all-knowing. How would it affect a person's life?

Further class and homework activities

1. Ask students to learn the Useful Words and their definitions as homework for a quick quiz next lesson.

2. Play 1.1 Audio Clip from the *Judaism OxBox Online* to the class. Ask students to mind-map everything that seems significant as they are listening. You could also ask, 'how does the Shema guide Jewish people on their relationship with God?'

3. Show 1.1 One God Film Clips A and B from the *Judaism Oxbox Online,* about the Reznik family's experiences of being close to God.

Ask students to share with a partner whether or not they believe in any kind of spiritual being. Ask for a student volunteer to feed back to the class.

4. 1.1 Film Worksheet on the *Judaism OxBox Online.*

5. 1.1 Attributes of God Interactive Activity on the *Judaism OxBox Online.*

6. Further suggestions on page 26 of this book.

1.2 How Does it Feel to be a Chosen People?

The unit in brief

This unit is about the belief, according to the Torah, that God chose the Jewish people to be a moral example, and to live righteously, justly and compassionately as role-models for the rest of humanity.

Key ideas

- Jewish people believe that they were chosen by God to be role-models for humanity
- The idea of being a chosen people may cause difficult issues amongst non-Jews
- Abraham was the 'father' of the Jewish nation

Useful Words

covenant, Chief Rabbi, Movements in Judaism, patriarch

Skills practised

- Literacy: preparing questions for a radio or TV interview
- Thinking: considering how the Jewish belief in being chosen could impact others
- Empathy: thinking about Abraham's feelings when he heard God's promise to him
- Reflection: reflecting on their own destiny and purpose in life

Resources

- 1.2 Chosen People Worksheet: Students reflect on how much of a 'light' they have been during one week
- 1.2 Abraham Interactive Activity: students select true statements about Abraham
- 1.2 Lesson Player: a ready-to-go presentation with built-in resources and teacher notes
- 1 Image Gallery: a useful gallery of photos and film stills from the chapter
- 1.2 Self-Assessment Sheet: students evaluate their learning against the lesson objectives

Ideas for starters

1. Use the Starter from the *Student Book*.
2. Discuss as a class, or in small groups, the possible positive and negative aspects of being chosen for a particular duty or purpose.
3. Ask the class what feelings might be generated in others towards a person who has been chosen.
4. Ask students, in pairs, to discuss whether they think they are a leader or a follower. They should compare the qualities involved in each.

Activity guidance

- The hot-seat activity in the *Student Book* (Activity 1) could be conducted as a class rather than pairs activity. It could be followed up by showing or handing out copies of an interview with Lord Jakobovitz (obtained from an Internet search).

- You could encourage students to identify the similarities and differences between the Jewish idea of being a chosen people and the Christian idea of being the 'body of Christ'. See Unit 3.2 in the *Christianity Student Book*.

Ideas for plenaries

1. Use the Reflection from the *Student Book*.

2. Ask the class why Jewish people believe they were chosen by God, and what issues might arise as a result of this belief.

3. Give students two minutes to tell a partner three qualities needed in someone who has been chosen for a responsible role.

4. Ask students to write down three behaviours expected of Jewish people when God chose them.

5. Ask students to think back over their actions during the day and identify examples of acting 'righteously, justly and compassionately'. Do they think it is easy or difficult to live in these ways all the time? Why?

Further class and homework activities

1. Ask students to write down the name of a person they look up to as a good example or role-model, and to say why. What qualities do they offer?

2. Ask a number of volunteers to write a word on the board describing the qualities they think are needed to be 'a moral guide and righteous leader'.

3. As a homework activity, ask students to create a written response to the Reflection in the *Student Book*, with reference to what they have learned in this unit.

4. 1.2 Chosen People Worksheet on the *Judaism OxBox Online*.

5. 1.2 Abraham Interactive Activity on the *Judaism OxBox Online*.

6. Further suggestions on page 26 of this book.

The unit in brief

This unit explores covenants between God and Jewish people. It uses four examples of key covenants from the Torah to show the nature of a covenant. God makes promises to the Jewish people with an expectation of righteous conduct in return. Signs are used to seal those covenants, for example Noah's rainbow.

Key ideas

- A covenant is an agreement, where something is promised in return for something else
- In Jewish covenants throughout history, God makes promises to the Jewish people in return for their righteous conduct
- Signs, like Noah's rainbow, are used to 'seal' covenants
- The Ten Commandments are part of God's covenant with the Jewish people through the story of Moses

Skills practised

- Analysis: identifying key features in a covenant story
- Thinking: responding to contrasting opinions about Noah's flood
- Research: researching and assessing four key figures from Jewish sacred texts
- Reflection: reflecting on the importance of outward signs as part of an agreement

Resources

- 1.3 Covenant Worksheet: Students analyse the covenants with Noah and Abraham

- 1.3 Covenant Interactive Activity: students complete sentences about covenants

- 1.3 Lesson Player: a ready-to-go presentation with built-in resources and teacher notes

- 1 Image Gallery: a useful gallery of photos and film stills from the chapter

- 1.3 Self-Assessment Sheet: students evaluate their learning against the lesson objectives

Ideas for starters

1. Use the Starter from the *Student Book*.

2. As a class discussion, ask what signs, symbols or gestures might be used to seal the deal in an agreement or promise. Ask students how important they think these are.

Activity guidance

For Activity 3 in the *Student Book*, you may need to explain that some Jews believe that the story of Noah is a historical event, whilst for others it is a metaphor for how Jews should live.

Ideas for plenaries

1. Use the Reflection from the *Student Book*.

2. Ask students to close their books and name the four main people from sacred texts mentioned in this unit.

3. Ask students to name two covenants where there were signs, and to explain what those signs were.

4. Ask what the covenants might tell us about God's relationship with the Jewish people.

5. Ask students to work with a partner to create a scenario where a covenant is being agreed. What promises and commitments will be made? What will they choose to symbolize their agreement? Share and discuss scenarios as a class.

Further class and homework activities

1. The research activity from the *Student Book* about Adam, Abraham, Moses and Noah could be set as a homework. Volunteers could then report back about each one in the next lesson.

2. Ask students to prepare to hot-seat the four main people from sacred texts mentioned in this unit, questioning them about their feelings and experiences of entering into a covenant with God on behalf of the Israelites.

3. 1.3 Covenant Worksheet on the *Judaism OxBox Online*.

4. 1.3 Covenant Interactive Activity on the *Judaism OxBox Online*.

5. Further suggestions on page 26 of this book.

The unit in brief

This unit introduces the idea of the Promised Land for the Jewish people. God made a covenant with the Israelites that the land of Canaan would be an everlasting inheritance to be passed on to the offspring of the Jewish people. The importance of Jerusalem as a place of sacred significance to Judaism is also introduced. Unit 5.5 covers this in more detail.

Key ideas

- The nomadic Jewish people are promised a permanent homeland
- God makes a covenant with the Israelites – land in exchange for loyalty and obedience
- Jerusalem is a sacred place to the Jewish faith

Useful Words

BCE, Canaan, exiled, King Solomon, Promised Land, sacrifices

Skills practised

- Thinking: considering what God's promise shows about His relationship with the Jewish people
- Literacy: writing two diary entries from a Jewish perspective
- Empathy: considering the possible reactions of the existing inhabitants to the arrival of the Jews in Canaan
- Reflection: reflecting on the significance of 'special places', for those with faith and those with secular world views

Resources

- 1.4 Audio Clip: a reading of Psalm 137:1–6
- 1.4 Promised Land Worksheet: Students complete sentences about the Promised Land
- 1.4 Promised Land Interactive Activity: students complete a paragraph about the Promised Land
- 1.4 Lesson Player: a ready-to-go presentation with built-in resources and teacher notes
- 1 Image Gallery: a useful gallery of photos and film stills from the chapter
- 1.4 Self-Assessment Sheet: students evaluate their learning against the lesson objectives

Ideas for starters

1. Use the Starter from the *Student Book*.

2. Ask the class if anybody knows what 'nomadic' means, and whether they can name any groups of people in the world today who still live nomadic lives.

3. Ask students what they think the impact might be of knowing that you have somewhere permanent to live.

4. Write the Unit heading on the board, or read it out. Tell the class that Israel is described a number of times in sacred texts as a land 'flowing with milk and honey'. Ask students what the images of milk and honey make them think about.

Activity guidance

Activity 3 in the *Student Book* could be presented as a blog, or an entry on a social media website.

Ideas for plenaries

1. Use the Reflection from the *Student Book*.

2. Ask students to explain why the Jewish people might be attracted to having a permanent homeland.

3. Ask students to explain the covenant that God made with the Jews about the Promised Land. What was promised and what was expected in return?

4. Ask why the Promised Land, and Jerusalem in particular, was important to the Jewish people.

5. Present students with the following scenario: 'Your best friend is going to celebrate his/her Bar or Bat Mitzvah in Jerusalem. What will you give as a present to mark this special occasion and why?'

6. Ask students to identify what makes a place sacred in no more than five words. Write these on sticky notes, display, and share.

Further class and homework activities

1. Show the class the following video clip from the BBC Learning Zone about the importance of Jerusalem for the Jews: www.bbc.co.uk/learningzone/clips/judaism-jews-and-the-holy-land. What questions do they have?

2. Play 1.4 Audio Clip on the *Judaism OxBox Online* to the class. Ask students to explain what this Psalm says about the importance of Jerusalem and the Promised Land to the Jewish people.

3. If you use the Starter activity in the *Student Book*, use 1 Image Gallery on the *Judaism OxBox Online* to have the Promised Land image available at the start of the lesson.

4. 1.4 Promised Land Worksheet on the *Judaism OxBox Online*.

5. 1.4 Promised Land Interactive Activity on the *Judaism OxBox Online*.

6. Further suggestions on page 26 of this book.

1.5 A Better World: The Messianic Age

The unit in brief

This unit is about a key belief in Orthodox Judaism that a wise and righteous leader, the Messiah (Mashiach), will emerge and bring about a perfect world. The Progressive Movement focuses on the idea that each person is responsible for creating a better world. Students explore the nature of leadership and the idea of a perfect future world.

Key ideas

- Judaism teaches of a better time to come: the Messianic Age
- Orthodox Jews believe the Messiah (Mashiach) will lead the Messianic Age
- According to sacred texts, the qualities and attributes of the Mashiach are righteous judge, observant Jew, and military leader
- Liberal and many Reform Jews do not believe there will be a 'chosen one', but rather that each person has a responsibility to create a better world

Useful Words

aleinu, tikkun olam

Skills practised

- Literacy: analysing the meaning of Torah quotes; writing a job advert for the Messiah
- Thinking: creating a written or visual response to the idea of a perfect world; responding to three philosophical statements
- Reflection: reflecting on the possibility and desirability of a perfect world

Resources

- 1.5 Messiah Age Worksheet: students decide whether or not sentences correctly describe the Messianic Age
- 1.5 Mashiach Interactive Activity: students identify attributes of the Mashiach according to sacred texts
- 1.5 Lesson Player: a ready-to-go presentation with built-in resources and teacher notes
- 1 Image Gallery: a useful gallery of photos and film stills from the chapter
- 1.5 Self-Assessment Sheet: students evaluate their learning against the lesson objectives

Ideas for starters

1. Use the Starter from the *Student Book*.

2. Show the class some photos of famous world leaders and ask what qualities these people might have in common.

3. Write the heading: 'Healing the World – Tikkun Olam' on the board. Invite students to add a word or phrase to describe what they think would need to change in order to heal our world.

4. Ask students to imagine a world that is perfect. What would be in it? What would not be in it?

Activity guidance

To help with Activity 1b in the *Student Book*, it might be useful to have some examples of suitable printed or online job advertisements available, to show how they can be presented and what qualities might be asked for from the candidate.

Ideas for plenaries

1. Use the Reflection from the *Student Book*.

2. Ask students to explain tikkun olam in their own words and then ask them to suggest two reasons why the world needs healing – what went wrong? Share and discuss as a class.

3. Doing your Bit! Ask students to think about what they could do themselves to contribute towards healing the world. They should share their ideas in pairs, then small groups, and finally feed back to the whole class.

4. Ask students to describe the Messianic Age.

5. 'It's no good hoping that everything will be better in a future, perfect world – humans have a responsibility to start putting things right now!' Discuss, and then vote on, this statement.

Further class and homework activities

1. As a class art project, a mural could be developed showing what the world might be like in the Messianic Age. Students could be asked, as homework, to design a stained glass window as preparation for this.

2. Activity 2 in the *Student Book* could also be set for homework.

3. As an extension exercise, some students could be asked to do more research into different Jewish perspectives on the Mashiach and Messianic Age. They could write three differing opinions in three speech bubbles as homework.

4. 1.5 Messianic Age Worksheet on the *Judaism OxBox Online*.

5. 1.5 Mashiach Interactive Activity on the *Judaism OxBox Online*.

6. Further suggestions on page 26 of this book.

Chapter 1 Further Suggestions

These suggestions are addressed directly to students.

1.1 There is Only One God

1   Write a letter to a rabbi asking him everything that puzzles you about God. *

2   Devise a role-play between a believer and a non-believer in one God. **

3   Design a logo for clothing which reminds the young Jewish wearer of God's attributes. *

4   With a partner, create a dialogue between an Orthodox Jewish person and someone who has lost belief owing to a terrible event. **

5   Memory Box – think of five objects to put in the box that would help a Jewish person think about God. *

6   Research different Jewish names for God. Make a decorative word-cloud with the names of the Jewish God. *

7   If God is all-loving, why might bad things happen? Write three paragraphs exploring arguments for and against, including your own and the Jewish viewpoint. ***

1.2 How Does it Feel to be a Chosen People?

1   In pairs, reflect on the people in school who hold positions of leadership, e.g. prefects, headgirl/boy, house captain, sports team captain, head teacher, caretaker, etc. What special qualities do they have? *

2   Write creatively (poetry, prose, dialogue) about your own or an imagined experience of being chosen for an important role and how it feels. **

3   Class vote: Best Footballer, Best Tennis Player, Best Politician, Best Member of the Royal Family. Reflect on those who gained the most votes. *

4   Destiny and Purpose – What is Yours? Form groups of three. Collaborate in creating individual segmented wheels with a photo of each group member in the centre. Write strengths and skills in the segments. *

5   Compare the Jewish experience of belonging to a chosen people with that of another faith, for example Christians as 'the body of Christ' or the sense of belonging to the Islamic community. ***

1.3 Covenants: Making a Deal With God

1   Find written examples of agreements/contracts. Summarize what was promised and what was expected in return. *

2   Role-play a dispute about a contract. *

3   In a small group, devise a contract (e.g. about Behaviour at Lunch time). What might be a sign to seal the deal? *

4   How might the nature of God be revealed through the covenants with Adam and Noah? ***

5   Look at the Ten Commandments in Exodus 20. Why are the Ten Commandments so important to the Jewish people? **

6   What might the Ten Commandments have to teach the wider world? **

7   Why might signs from God be important to Jews? **

1.4 A Land Flowing With Milk and Honey

1   Using the Internet, in pairs, research sacred places in Israel. Why are they special and what happens there? *

2   Write creatively (prose/poetry/dialogue) about a special place to you, focusing on what happens there/why it is special/how you feel when you are there. **

3   Why does it matter so much that every people, community or family has a sense that somewhere is their home or their 'place'? What would be the implications of not having such a place? ***

1.5 A Better World: the Messianic Age

1   Divide the class into groups of four. Decide on three students to be on an interview panel and one student to be a candidate. Devise interview questions to find out if the candidate has the right qualities to be the Messiah. Conduct the interview. **

2   In small groups, devise a questionnaire entitled Doing Your Bit. Focus on small ways you can change behaviour or do good deeds to help heal the world. This could be developed into a cross-class School Project. Carry out your questionnaire and present your results. **

3   Do some research to find out what other faiths teach about a perfect future world (for example, the Christian idea of heaven, or Islamic paradise). Identify and discuss similarities and differences. Why do you think so many people are hoping for a perfect world? ***

4   Prepare for a debate on the statement: 'It's better to work on improving the world we have than to hope for a perfect world in the future.' ***

Chapter 1 Assessment

Assessment in the *Student Book*

You will find an assessment task at the end of every chapter which focuses on AT2. In this chapter, the task asks students to write a work appraisal for the God worshipped by the Jews.

In the *Student Book* (and on the supporting worksheets), you'll find guidance about levels of assessment that you can use to help your students understand what their work should include. You could ask them to use these criteria for self- or peer-assessment once they've completed the task.

Assessment Task for Chapter 1 (pages **18–19** of the *Judaism Student Book*)

Objectives

- Apply Jewish beliefs about the nature of God.
- Reflect on the challenges of a belief in the attributes of the Jewish God.

Task

Evaluate the work of God! Try to evaluate what you have learned about God, according to Jewish beliefs. Write a work appraisal for the God worshipped by Jews. It needs to include:
- personal attributes (for example, all-present)
- previous work experience (for example, creating the world)
- the ability to select able individuals to work for Him (for example, Moses)
- the achievement of aims and objectives
- the ability to forecast.

Assessment in *OxBox Online*

On the *Judaism OxBox Online*, you'll find resources to use when introducing the assessment task to the class.

You can use the *Chapter 1 Assessment Task Presentation* as a front-of-class tool to help your students unpack the assessment criteria, and understand what is expected of them.

Chapter 1 Assessment Worksheets accompany the task, so that once you finish the presentation, your students can easily get started.

Auto-marked tests

The *Judaism OxBox Online* also contains auto-marked tests for each chapter to help save you time setting questions and marking for AT1. The test for this chapter contains 15 questions and will take most students about half an hour. Test results are automatically stored in the markbook.

Digital markbook

A markbook and a reporting function complete the *OxBox Online* assessment package, so you can keep all your students' test results and assessment scores in one place. This can include the auto-marked tests as well as pieces of work you or the students have marked by hand.

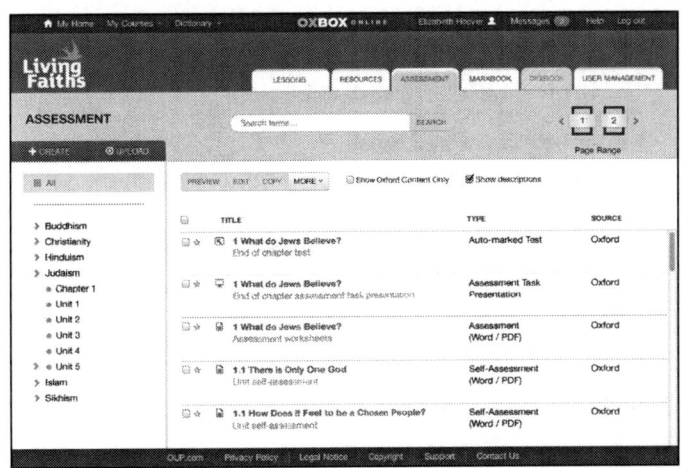

▲ Assessment resources for Chapter 1 on the *Judaism Oxbox Online*

Chapter 2 Overview
Where do Jewish Beliefs Come From?

Helping you deliver Key Stage 3 RE

This chapter addresses the following areas of the Programme of Study:

Key concepts

Beliefs, teachings and sources
- Interpreting teachings, sources, authorities (including the Torah) and ways of life in order to understand religions and beliefs

Practices and ways of life
- Understanding that religious practices are diverse, change over time and are influenced by cultures

Key processes

Learning about religion
- Investigate the impact of religious beliefs and teachings on individuals, communities and societies, the reasons for commitment and the causes of diversity
- Explain religious beliefs, practices and commitments, including their transmission by people, texts and traditions
- Interpret a range of sources, texts, authorities, and forms of religious and spiritual expression from a variety of contexts

Learning from religion
- Reflect on the relationship between beliefs, teachings, world issues and ultimate questions
- Express students' own beliefs and ideas, using a variety of forms of expression, including creative forms and reasoned arguments

The big picture

These are the key ideas behind this chapter:

- There are three sections to the Tanakh including Torah, Nevi'im and Ketuvim.
- Orthodox Jews believe the Torah is given by God to the Jewish people.
- Prophets and Writings are believed to be written by man but with God's inspiration.
- The Talmud is a guidebook to the Torah.
- God commanded the Exodus story to be told from generation to generation. This is expressed in the Hagadah.

- Throughout the centuries rabbis have interpreted and commented on sacred texts and influenced Jewish practice.

Chapter outline

Use this to give students a mental road-map of the chapter:

2.1 How is the Torah Special? – introduces the most important sacred text in Judaism

2.2 Mitzvot: Rules to Live by – explains the significance of mitzvot (rules) in the lives of Jewish people

2.3 Nevi'im: Prophetic Stories, Warnings and Promises – introduces the range of literature in the Nevi'im, which is part of the Tanakh

2.4 Ketuvim: Psalms, Proverbs ... and More Stories! – identifies the range of literature in Ketuvim, which is part of the Tanakh

2.5 The Talmud – A Guidebook for Jewish Living – explains the significance of a book which helps to make sense of the Torah

2.6 Passover: Why is This Night Different From All Other Nights? – explores how Jews fulfil the commandment to tell the story of the exodus to their children including the importance of Hagadah

2.7 Judaism in a Changing World: What do the Rabbis Say? – examines the views of rabbis and how they have influenced Jewish belief and practice

Opportunities for assessment

Summative assessments on the *Judaism OxBox Online* include automarked tests, interactive activities, and self-assessment worksheets.

The end-of-chapter assessment task in the *Student Book* provides formative assessment. Supporting materials for the assessment task can be found on the *Judaism OxBox Online*, such as the Assessment Task Presentation and the related worksheets.

There are other opportunities for assessment too. For example, you could use some of the activities or reflection points throughout each *Student Book* unit, or some of the 'Further Suggestions' at the end of this chapter.

Getting ready for this chapter

- If you have the *Judaism OxBox Online,* watch the case study film clips in advance, so that you can prepare and guide students before and during their viewing.

Objectives and outcomes for this chapter

Objectives	Unit	Outcomes
Most students will:		Most students will be able to:
• analyse the significance of the Torah for Jewish people • learn how Jewish people show love and respect for the Torah • reflect on what makes the Torah special.	2.1	• use key terms to explain why the Torah is so important in Judaism • give examples of how love and respect are shown to the Torah • identify what makes the Torah special.
• analyse the significance of mitzvot (commandments) for Jewish people • learn how these commandments can be interpreted by different Movements in Judaism • reflect on the role and importance of rules in daily life.	2.2	• explain the importance of mitzvot to Jewish people and how they affect daily living • identify different attitudes across the Jewish spectrum to these rules • debate the role and importance of rules in daily life.
• identify the range of literature in Nevi'im and why they are important • evaluate the significance of prophetic stories, warnings and promises • reflect on, and respond to, a story from Nevi'im.	2.3	• give examples of different forms of writing found in Nevi'im • state what might be important about prophetic stories, warnings and promises • explain some issues a story from Nevi'im might make us think about.
• identify the range of literature in Ketuvim • consider the idea of Ketuvim being divinely inspired • reflect on and respond to a particular Psalm, Proverb and story from Ketuvim.	2.4	• give examples of different forms of writing in Ketuvim • explain the meaning of 'divinely inspired' and the impact of this when reading Ketuvim • describe their response to the ideas in a particular Psalm, Proverb and story.
• explain the form and role of the Talmud • evaluate the impact of the Talmud on Jewish life today • reflect on who or what you turn to when something is hard to understand.	2.5	• describe the content and role of the Talmud using key terms • state how the Talmud might influence Jewish people • debate how to find meaning and clarity when something is hard to understand.
• explore the story of the first Pesach (Passover) • analyse the role and importance of the Hagadah at the Passover Seder • reflect on the importance of freedom for yourself and others.	2.6	• give an account of the story of Passover • explain the form of the Hagadah and how it is used in the Passover Seder • debate the importance of freedom to Jews and non-Jews.
• examine the views of rabbis from different Movements in interpreting Jewish law and practice • respond to people from different Jewish Movements • reflect on the idea of spiritual honesty.	2.7	• identify areas of Jewish practice that have been influenced by the thinking of rabbis across the Jewish spectrum • ask some questions about the thoughts and experiences of families from different Jewish Movements • explain what might be meant by spiritual honesty.

2.1 How is the Torah Special?

The unit in brief

This unit considers the central importance of the Torah to Judaism, through the perspectives of Jewish families from different Movements.

Key ideas

- The Torah contains the Five Books of Moses (Genesis, Exodus, Leviticus, Numbers, and Deuteronomy)
- The Torah contains the Written Law
- The Torah can be recorded in both book form and as a scroll (Sefer Torah)
- The Jewish people show great love and respect for the Torah in a number of ways

Useful Words

Ark, rabbi, Reform Judaism

Skills practised

- Literacy: identifying differences between Jewish Movements from quotations
- Thinking: creating a poster to apply Jewish ideas about the Torah
- Reflection: reflecting on the 'specialness' of certain books like the Torah and others

Resources

- ⎍⎍ 2.1 Audio Clip: a recording of the Eitz Chaim prayer
- ▦ 2.1 Torah Film Clip A: Jordan and Mr Reznik talk about the importance of the Torah
- ▦ 2.1 Torah Film Clip B: Shuli Morris explains why the Torah is special to her
- 🗎 2.1 Film Worksheet: students assess their understanding of the case study film clips by linking ideas to the
- ⬉ 2.1 Torah Interactive Activity: students select true statements about the Torah
- 🏠 2.1 Lesson Player: a ready-to-go presentation with built-in resources and teacher notes
- 🖳 2 Image Gallery: a useful gallery of photos and film stills from the chapter
- 🗎 2.1 Self-Assessment Sheet: students evaluate their learning against the lesson objectives

Ideas for starters

1. Use the Starter from the *Student Book*.

2. Ask students to say who or what guides them in their decisions about right and wrong.

3. Ask the class why they think sacred books are considered important.

4. Ask what makes a sacred book different from any other book.

Activity guidance

- In response to the activity related to Shifra Morris's quotation in the *Student Book*, students could mention the stories of: Noah's Ark, Moses and the Red Sea, Joseph and his coat.

- Show students example photos of different Torah mantles prior to their attempting Activity 1 in the *Student Book*.

Ideas for plenaries

1. Use the Reflection from the .

2. Ask students to close their books and then write down the names of the Five Books of Moses in the Torah.

3. Ask why the Torah is so important to Jewish people.

4. Ask students to describe the ways in which Jewish people show love and respect for the Torah.

5. Ask students to discuss in pairs what authorities they would obey and why. Share as a class. Are there some authorities they would not submit to? Why?

Further class and homework activities

1. As homework, ask students to create a comic strip showing the steps involved in being called up to read from the Torah (as outlined by Mr Reznik in the *Student Book*).

2. Ask higher ability students what they think the impact might be of believing that the Torah is the actual word of God and cannot be changed by humanity. Ask them to compare this idea with the Islamic attitude to the Qur'an, if they are also studying Islam.

3. Show 2.1 Torah Film Clips A and B on the *Judaism OxBox Online* to illustrate different interpretations of the Torah from Orthodox and Reform Judaism.

4. 2.1 Film Worksheet on the *Judaism OxBox Online*.

5. 2.1 Torah Interactive Activity on the *Judaism OxBox Online*.

6. 2.1 Audio Clip on the *Judaism OxBox Online*.

7. Further suggestions on page 44 of this book.

2.2 Mitzvot: Rules to Live by

The unit in brief

This unit introduces the idea that, scattered throughout the Torah, are 613 rules (mitzvot) from God. Case study examples are used to consider differences in the interpretation of mitzvot within different Jewish Movements, and how they relate to modern living.

Key ideas

- There are 613 mitzvot throughout the Torah.
- The mitzvot affect all aspects of Jewish life.
- Mitzvot are interpreted by the Talmud.
- Attitudes to mitzvot vary, according to the different Jewish Movements.

Useful Words

Liberal Judaism, Progressive Judaism, Talmud

Skills practised

- Literacy: writing 'A day in the life of an Orthodox Jew'; writing creatively about a world without rules
- Thinking: considering the attitudes of different Jewish Movements to the following of mitzvot
- Research: finding out more about different mitzvot
- Reflection: reflecting on the role of rules in daily life

Resources

- 2.2 Mitzvot Film Clip A: Laurie and Jordan Reznik talk about why they believe mitzvot are important
- 2.2 Mitzvot Film Clip B: Hollie Walton explains her attitude to mitzvot and how she makes decisions about right and wrong
- 2.2 Film Worksheet: students assess their understanding of the case study film clips by linking ideas to the *Student Book*
- 2.2 Mitzvot Interactive Activity: students complete sentences about mitzvot
- 2.2 Lesson Player: a ready-to-go presentation with built-in resources and teacher notes
- 2 Image Gallery: a useful gallery of photos and film stills from the chapter
- 2.2 Self-Assessment Sheet: students evaluate their learning against the lesson objectives

Activity guidance

- Hold a class debate about students' responses to the Reflection activity in the *Student Book*. You could also ask them to explain their opinions in more detail as homework.

- You could compare Jewish attitudes to rules with other faiths. See Unit 2.5 in the *Hinduism Student Book*, or Unit 2.4 in the *Islam Student Book*.

Ideas for plenaries

1. Use the Reflection from the *Student Book*.

2. Ask students to describe in their own words what mitzvot are and where they come from.

3. Oscar Nominations! Ask students to decide on the most interesting, surprising, and most difficult to understand fact about mitzvot.

4. Ask the class to vote on whether they would prefer a world with rules or without. Ask a selection of students to justify their opinions.

2.3 Nevi'im: Prophetic Stories, Warnings and Promises

The unit in brief

This unit is about Nevi'im (Prophets) – one of the three sections of the sacred text (the Tanakh). It focuses on the prophetic literature in Nevi'im, using the example of the story of the Prophet Jonah.

Key ideas

- The Tanakh is in three sections: Torah, Nevi'im and Ketuvim
- Prophets were sent warnings and promises from God to give to the Jewish people, as recorded in Nevi'im
- Stories, poetry and song can inspire teaching, learning and spiritual experiences

Useful Words

prophets, Yom Kippur

Skills practised

- Literacy: writing a speech to the people of Nineveh
- Thinking: considering the messages that can be taken from the story of Jonah
- Reflection: reflecting on why some people turn to God in times of trouble

Resources

- 📄 2.3 Jonah Worksheet: students fill in a story board for Jonah
- ⬚ 2.3 Tanakh Interactive Activity: students decide whether statements about the Tanakh are true or false
- 🏠 2.3 Lesson Player: a ready-to-go presentation with built-in resources and teacher notes
- 🖥 2 Image Gallery: a useful gallery of photos and film stills from the chapter
- 📄 2.3 Self-Assessment Sheet: students evaluate their learning against the lesson objectives

Ideas for starters

1. Use the Starter from the *Student Book*.
2. If you have a copy of the Tanakh available, demonstrate that it is divided into three sections, and look in particular at the books from Nevi'im.
3. Ask students whether or not they listen to warnings. Then ask what they know about the story of Jonah.
4. Ask students how they think different forms like stories, songs and poems might help us to understand certain teachings. Do they make learning easier or harder?

Activity guidance

The Jonah story would be an ideal opportunity for a community of enquiry. Three philosophical questions have already been provided in Activity 1 of the *Student Book* for students to discuss. Ideally, students could generate their own questions and vote on which ones they would like to discuss in groups.

Ideas for plenaries

1. Use the Reflection from the *Student Book*.

2. Ask students to think of examples of stories, poetry and songs that inspire or prompt spiritual responses.

3. Ask students to prepare questions to hot-seat Jonah – with the teacher taking on the role. Encourage students to explore Jonah's feelings at each stage of the story.

4. What does the story of Jonah teach about the forgiveness of God and how far it goes?

5. Ask students to find an example where they, or someone they know, was forced to do something they didn't want to do. What similarities and differences are there with the story of Jonah?

Further class and homework activities

1. As homework, ask students to write an explanation of how the story of Jonah can be seen as prophetic. What can they learn from the story about the characteristics of a prophet?

2. Ask students, in pairs, to create a pop-up book to tell the story of Jonah to young children. They should think carefully about which parts of the story should be emphasized.

3. 2.3 Jonah Worksheet on the *Judaism OxBox Online*.

4. 2.3 Tanakh Interactive Activity on the *Judaism OxBox Online*.

5. Further suggestions on page 44 of this book.

2.4 Ketuvim: Psalms, Proverbs ... and More Stories!

The unit in brief

This unit is about one of the three sections, Ketuvim (Writings), in the Tanakh. Ketuvim is Hebrew literature in the form of poems (like the Psalms), stories, wise sayings (Proverbs) and songs. An example of a Psalm, Proverb and story is included to allow for reflection on form and meaning.

Key ideas

- Ketuvim (Writings) is one of the three sections in the Tanakh
- Ketuvim consist of literature in several forms
- The writings are believed to be divinely inspired
- It is believed that King David wrote the majority of the 150 Psalms
- Psalm 121, Proverbs 24:17 and the story of Ruth are explored in detail

Useful Words

Megillot, Ruach Hakodesh

Skills practised

- Literacy: analysing a Psalm, Proverb and story in detail
- Thinking: creating a role-play to put across a message in a modern context
- Research: researching the life of King David
- Reflection: reflecting on the meaning of divinely inspired poetry

Resources

- ⌇ 2.4 Audio Clip: a reading of Psalm 121

- 🗎 2.4 Psalm Worksheet: students read through Psalm 121 and answer questions on it

- ⬉ 2.4 Ketuvim Interactive Activity: students complete a paragraph about Ketuvim

- 🏠 2.4 Lesson Player: a ready-to-go presentation with built-in resources and teacher notes

- 🖳 2 Image Gallery: a useful gallery of photos and film stills from the chapter

- 🗎 2.4 Self-Assessment Sheet: students evaluate their learning against the lesson objectives

Ideas for starters

1. Use the Starter from the *Student Book*.

2. Write an example of a promise from Psalm 121 on the board, e.g. 'The Lord will guard you from all harm'. Ask students whether they believe in promises like this. Ask them to explain their opinions.

3. Ask students what they already know about Psalms and Proverbs.

Activity guidance

For Activity 1 in the *Student Book*, you may wish to direct students to certain websites, for example the Jewish Virtual Library.

Ideas for plenaries

1. Use the Reflection from the *Student Book*.

2. Ask five student volunteers to stand in a circle in front of the class. Each volunteer should take it in turns to throw a soft ball to one of the other volunteers, who then has to name any literature from Ketuvim.

3. Ask students to discuss in pairs what the effect might be of hearing Psalms (sometimes put to music).

4. Read Psalm 23 to the class. Tell them it is often read or sung at funerals. Why do they think this is?

5. 'Although the Proverbs and wise sayings were written thousands of years ago, their teachings still apply to today's world because human nature hasn't really changed.' Ask students whether they agree or disagree, and ask them to explain why, using examples from the unit or their research to support their argument.

Further class and homework activities

1. Activity 1 in the *Student Book* could be completed as homework.

2. It is often said that, whatever feelings people have, they can be found expressed somewhere in the Psalms. As homework, ask students to do some research to explore some of the most popular Psalms and identify the feelings and emotions expressed.

3. Ask students to read Proverbs 3 and choose the proverb they think is the most useful for their own lives. Ask them to explain their decision.

4. Ask students to find examples in Psalm 121 where God has been written about in human terms. How might this Psalm bring comfort? What questions would you ask the writer if you could?

5. 2.4 Psalm Worksheet on the *Judaism OxBox Online*.

6. 2.4 Ketuvim Interactive Activity on the *Judaism OxBox Online*.

7. 2.4 Audio Clip on the *Judaism OxBox Online*.

8. Further suggestions on page 44 of this book.

2.5 The Talmud: A Guidebook for Jewish Living

The unit in brief

This unit introduces students to the Talmud as a guidebook to help understand Jewish law and practice. A significant area of Jewish life (Shabbat observance) is used as an example of how the Talmud interprets the Torah.

Key ideas

- God communicated with Moses in two different ways, which resulted in the Written Torah and Oral Torah
- The Oral Law of the Talmud helps to explain and interpret the Written Torah
- The Talmud is divided into two parts: the Mishnah (six areas of living) and the Gemara (more detailed interpretations)

Skills practised

- Literacy: devising a questionnaire about work
- Thinking: considering whether it's a good idea to modernize ancient rules; debating a statement
- Reflection: reflecting on where to go for guidance when something is hard to understand

Resources

- 📄 2.1 Talmud Worksheet: students analyse a small section from the Talmud about Shabbat
- 🖱 2.1 Talmud Interactive Activity: students link key terms from the unit with their definitions
- 🏠 2.1 Lesson Player: a ready-to-go presentation with built-in resources and teacher notes
- 🖥 2 Image Gallery: a useful gallery of photos and film stills from the chapter
- 📄 2.1 Self-Assessment Sheet: students evaluate their learning against the lesson objectives

Ideas for starters

1. Use the Starter from the *Student Book*.

2. Show students examples of guidebooks, such as travel guides (or guides to historic buildings like castles or cathedrals). Ask them to discuss the purpose of guidebooks in small groups and then feed back their ideas to the class.

3. Show the class a picture of an abstract painting that could be interpreted in a number of different ways. Ask students what they think the painting might mean – how it could be interpreted. Hold a class discussion about the notion of interpretation.

Activity guidance

- Students could use the questionnaires they prepared for Activity 2 in the *Student Book* to conduct a survey about people's opinions.

- Activity 3 in the *Student Book* could move from a small group to a whole-class debate, with a spokesperson representing each group.

Ideas for plenaries

1. Use the Reflection from the *Student Book*.

2. Hold a class discussion about why and how a guidebook to Jewish sacred texts might be helpful.

3. Ask students which areas they might include if they were writing a guidebook about modern day-to-day living. What differences, if any, are there from the areas covered by the Talmud?

4. Give students the following verse from the Torah and ask them to discuss in small groups how it could be interpreted:
   'A woman must not put on man's apparel, nor shall a man wear woman's clothing...' (Deuteronomy 22:5).

5. Ask students to explain what a Yeshiva is.

Further class and homework activities

1. As homework, ask students to conduct a survey using their questionnaires from Activity 2 in the *Student Book*. Feed back the results of the survey next lesson.

2. 2.5 Talmud Worksheet on the *Judaism OxBox Online*.

3. 2.5 Talmud Interactive Activity on the *Judaism OxBox Online*.

4. Further suggestions on page 44 of this book.

2.6 Passover: Why is This Night Different From All Other Nights?

The unit in brief

This unit uses case studies to explain the Jewish spring festival of Passover (Pesach). There is a focus on the Torah commanding adults to tell their children the story of the exodus from slavery in Egypt. This takes place during the Seder, reading from the Hagadah.

Key ideas

- There is a commandment in the Torah to tell the story of the exodus from slavery in Egypt to the next generation
- To celebrate, Jewish people have a Passover Seder service and meal
- The book from which the exodus story is told is called the Hagadah

Skills practised

- Literacy: writing a book for young children to explain the Passover story
- Thinking: considering the importance of passing information across generations
- Research: researching the four questions which Jewish children have to ask at Passover
- Reflection: reflecting on the value and importance of freedom

Resources

- 2.6 Audio Clip: the singing of the four questions at Passover seder
- 2.6 Passover Film Clip A: The Reznik family share how they celebrate the Passover festival together
- 2.6 Passover Film Clip B: The Reznik family continue to share how they celebrate the Passover festival together
- 2.6 Film Worksheet: students assess their understanding of the case study film clip by linking ideas to the *Student Book*
- 2.6 Passover Interactive Activity: students complete sentences about Passover
- 2.6 Lesson Player: a ready-to-go presentation with built-in resources and teacher notes
- 2 Image Gallery: a useful gallery of photos and film stills from the chapter
- 2.6 Self-Assessment Sheet: students evaluate their learning against the lesson objectives

Ideas for starters

1. Use the Starter from the *Student Book*.

2. Ask students to discuss, in small groups, any stories they can remember which may have helped them to understand something difficult.

3. Ask for volunteers to tell the class about any important family stories which may have been passed down to them from previous generations. Do they know how far back the story goes?

4. Ask students to discuss in pairs how our own history might be preserved.

Activity guidance

Before exploring the Passover festival in detail, you may wish to work through the story of the escape of the Jews from Egypt in Exodus 12. Exploring this will provide context and enable students to understand why it is a story Jewish people want to pass on to the next generation, in response to God's commandment.

Ideas for plenaries

1. Use the Reflection from the *Student Book*.

2. Ask students to write three phrases on a sticky note to describe the power of a good story:

   - A good story is…
   - A good story has…
   - A good story makes you…

3. Ask why Jewish people must keep retelling the Passover story.

4. Ask why children are so central to the Hagadah.

5. What would life be like if there were no stories?

Further class and homework activities

1. Ask students to conduct some research and then explain to each other, in pairs, the meanings of the symbolic food on the Seder plate. Ask students, in pairs, to create a 'menu' card of the order of the Passover Seder.

2. Show 2.6 Passover Film Clips A and B on the *Judaism Oxbox Online* to the class.

3. 2.6 Film Worksheet on the *Judaism OxBox Online*.

4. 2.6 Audio Clip on the *Judaism OxBox Online*.

5. 2.6 Passover Interactive Activity on the *Judaism OxBox Online*.

6. Further suggestions on page 44 of this book.

2.7 Judaism in a Changing World: What do the Rabbis Say?

The unit in brief

This unit introduces students to the influence and role of rabbis in interpreting Jewish law and practice. Students reflect on how Movements have responded to the challenges of modernity. Beliefs about the spirit and letter of the law are considered.

Key ideas

- Rabbis question, debate and interpret matters of Jewish law and practice
- Different interpretations have led to the development of different Movements within Judaism
- Modernity has impacted Judaism in a number of ways, for example the role of girls and women

Useful Words

Halakhah, rabbi

Skills practised

- Literacy: writing questions to ask an Orthodox rabbi
- Thinking: considering points to be made in a debate about a particular statement
- Research: researching the views and influence of rabbis from different Movements
- Reflection: reflecting on what 'spiritual honesty' means

Resources

- 2.7 Rabbi Film Clip A: The Walton family talk about the role of Rabbis in Liberal Judaism
- 2.7 Rabbi Film Clip B: The Morris family talk about their female Rabbi
- 2.7 Film Worksheet: students assess their understanding of the case study film clips by linking ideas to the *Student Book*
- 2.7 Movements Interactive Activity: students complete a paragraph about Movements in Judaism
- 2.7 Lesson Player: a ready-to-go presentation with built-in resources and teacher notes
- 2 Image Gallery: a useful gallery of photos and film stills from the chapter
- 2.7 Self-Assessment Sheet: students evaluate their learning against the lesson objectives

Ideas for starters

1. Use the Starter from the *Student Book*.

2. Ask students, in pairs, to discuss two experiences that could be interpreted in different ways.

3. Ask students to think about an area of Jewish practice that might be influenced by different interpretations, e.g. observing Shabbat (see Unit 2.5). Ask them to vote on the following questions:
   - Should practice remain the same or change?
   - What are the advantages of things remaining the same?
   - What are the disadvantages?

4. Ask students, in pairs, to think of six modern devices that might interfere with strict Shabbat observance. (If necessary, refer students back to Unit 2.5.)

Activity guidance

- For Activity 1 in the *Student Book*, you could divide up the list of rabbis between the different groups, to ensure that at least one group researches each rabbi listed.

- After students have completed Activity 3 in the *Student Book*, you may wish to debate the statement as a class or in small groups.

Ideas for plenaries

1. Use the Reflection from the *Student Book*.

2. Ask students to pair, share and feed back on the question: 'If God made the laws, how can humanity change them?'

3. Ask students to devise a question for each of the family members featured in this unit.

4. Ask them which Jewish Movement they might feel most comfortable being a member of and why.

Further class and homework activities

1. As homework, ask students to use the Internet to research two more Jewish Movements – Charedi and Masorti. They should write a mission statement for each Movement.

2. Show 2.7 Rabbi Film Clips A and B on the *Judaism Oxbox Online*. Ask students, in pairs, to summarize what they have learned.

3. 2.7 Film Worksheet on the *Judaism OxBox Online*.

4. 2.7 Movements Interactive Activity on the *Judaism OxBox Online*.

5. Further suggestions on page 44 of this book.

Chapter 2 Further Suggestions

These suggestions are addressed directly to students.

2.1 Why is the Torah Special?

1   Imagine you have set up an interview with a Rabbi. Devise at least five questions to ask him or her about the Torah. *

2   Find a story from the Torah, for example David and Goliath or Joseph and his coat. Re-write it as if it were happening in modern times. **

3   Make a Torah scroll. On the 'parchment' write the names of the Five Books of Moses and their names in Hebrew. *

4   Design a Torah mantle (cover) with appropriate symbols to reflect the importance of the Torah for Jewish people. **

2.2 Mitzvot: Rules to Live by

1   With a partner, devise new school rules taking into account: justice; relationships (between teachers and students, students and teachers, students and students); care of the environment. *

2   Debate this statement: Most of the Jewish mitzvot do not apply to the modern world. ***

3   Journal entry: A Day in a Life Without Rules. How many mitzvot can he/she break? **

4   Judge and Jury: Put on trial the man/woman who wrote the Journal (above). Create a jury from 12 volunteers. **

2.3 Nevi'im: Prophetic Stories, Warnings and Promises

1   With a partner, using the Nevi'im section of the Tanakh and information from the Internet, research the prophetess Deborah in Judges 4. Devise a PowerPoint presentation about her for the class. ***

2   Design a Poster aimed to help find Jonah who has gone missing. Last Seen … *

3   Write a journal entry/blog of a day in the belly of a big fish from the point of view of Jonah. **

2.4 Ketuvim: Psalms, Proverbs … and More Stories!

1   There are 150 Psalms found in the Ketuvim section of the Tanakh. Find one you particularly like. Choose a few lines which you think would be particularly meaningful for a Jewish person and create a bookmark with the words inscribed. *

2   Take a walk through the Book of Proverbs in Ketuvim! Choose seven wise sayings and make a pocket book for every day of the week containing each of your chosen sayings. Illustrate each page. **

3   Draw a time-line for the life of King David (researching information on the Internet). *

4   Choose one wise saying with a powerful message for modern times from Proverbs to use as a poster on a double-decker bus. Why have you chosen this? How could it impact the world? ***

2.5 The Talmud: A Guidebook for Jewish Living

1   With a partner, using the Internet, find out three key facts about Gemara. *

2   Imagine interviewing a man studying at a Yeshiva. With a partner, devise interview questions about the experience/how the day is spent, etc. *

3   Role-play a debate about an area of living expressed in Torah. Example: observing Shabbat. **

4   Make a PowerPoint which explains in very clear terms what the Talmud is, and why it is important to Jewish people. ***

2.6 Passover: Why is This Night Different From All Other Nights?

1   Devise a rhyme or jingle for young children to help remember the Passover story. *

2   Using a copy of the Hagadah, in a small group, choose a scribe to write an order to the seder service. **

3   Create a beautiful and decorative front cover for a Hagadah with appropriate symbols. Be prepared to explain your decisions. ***

2.7 Judaism in a Changing World: What do the Rabbis Say?

1   Research Charedi (ultra-Orthodox) Judaism. What makes it different from other Movements? Devise a PowerPoint with your findings. **

2   Puzzles! Write a reflection about what puzzles you in this unit. *

3   Imagine you are a researcher for a TV programme about both the rabbis pictured on page 32 of the *Student Book*. Your task is to prepare a short introduction to each rabbi, explaining their main contributions to Jewish thinking. **

Chapter 2 Assessment

Assessment in the *Student Book*

You will find an assessment task at the end of every chapter which focuses on AT2. In this chapter, the task asks students to prepare a 20-minute lesson about the Torah, using a variety of creative teaching methods.

In the *Student Book* (and on the supporting worksheets), you'll find guidance about levels of assessment that you can use to help your students understand what their work should include. You could ask them to use these criteria for self- or peer-assessment once they've completed the task.

Living Faiths Assessment

Student Book
- Assessment Task
- Levels Guidance

OxBox Online
- Auto-Marked Test
- Assessment Task Presentation
- Assessment Worksheets

Assessment Task for Chapter 2 (pages **34–35** of the *Judaism Student Book*)

Objectives

- Explore the nature of key Jewish sacred texts.
- Evaluate the role of sacred texts in Judaism.
- Assess the impacts of those sacred texts on Jewish beliefs.

Task

Become teachers for a day! In pairs, prepare a 20-minute lesson about the Torah. It should aim to be understandable and enjoyable for students who know very little about Judaism. Be creative! Use a range of resources and teaching methods to enable your audience to engage fully with the learning experience.

Assessment in *OxBox Online*

On the *Judaism OxBox Online*, you'll find resources to use when introducing the assessment task to the class.

You can use the *Chapter 2 Assessment Task Presentation* as a front-of-class tool to help your students unpack the assessment criteria, and understand what is expected of them.

Chapter 2 Assessment Worksheets accompany the task, so that once you finish the presentation, your students can easily get started.

Auto-marked tests

The *Judaism OxBox Online* also contains auto-marked tests for each chapter to help save you time setting questions and marking for AT1. The test for this chapter contains 15 questions and will take most students about half an hour. Test results are automatically stored in the markbook.

Digital markbook

A markbook and a reporting function complete the *OxBox Online* assessment package, so you can keep all your students' test results and assessment scores in one place. This can include the auto-marked tests as well as pieces of work you or the students have marked by hand.

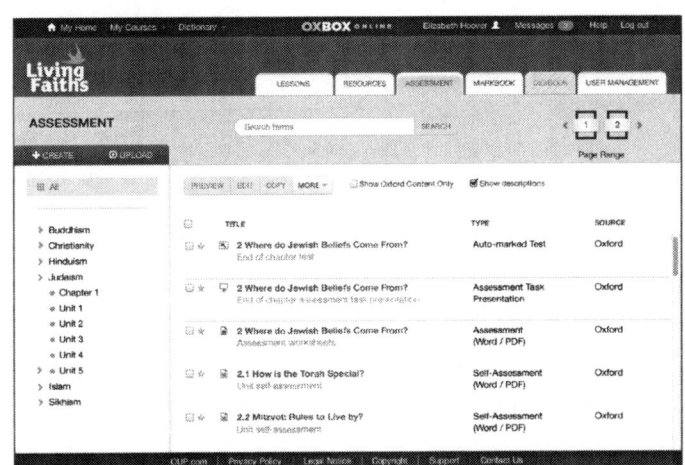

▲ Assessment resources for Chapter 2 on the *Judaism Oxbox Online*

Belonging to the Jewish Faith

Helping you deliver Key Stage 3 RE
This chapter addresses the following areas of the Programme of Study:

Key concepts
Practices and ways of life
- Exploring the impact of religions and beliefs on how people live their lives
- Understanding that religious practices are diverse, change over time and are influenced by cultures

Expressing meaning
- Appreciating that individuals and cultures express their beliefs and values through many different forms

Identity, diversity and belonging
- Understanding how individuals develop a sense of identity and belonging through faith or belief

Key processes
Learning about religion
- Investigate the impact of religious beliefs and teachings on individuals, communities and societies
- Explain religious beliefs, practices and commitments, including their transmission by people, texts and traditions

Learning from religion
- Evaluate beliefs, commitments and the impact of religion in the contemporary world

The big picture
These are the key ideas behind this chapter:

- Shabbat (Sabbath) is important for Jewish people. It is a day of rest from work. Jewish Movements interpret 'work' in different ways.
- Kashrut laws are Jewish food laws. For Orthodox Jews in particular, there are laws in the Torah about food preparation and forbidden foods that they follow strictly.
- Judaism has many festivals, including Sukkot, Purim and Rosh Hashanah.
- Bar and Bat Mitzvah are coming-of-age ceremonies for Jewish young people between 12 and 13.

Chapter outline
Use this to give students a mental road-map of the chapter:

3.1 Shabbat: A Special Day – introduces the different ways Jewish people interpret the commandment to rest on the Sabbath day

3.2 Let's Think Food – covers the laws of kashrut, what it means to 'keep kosher' and how food is prepared

3.3 Synagogues in the Community – introduces synagogues as centres of worship, prayer and community activity

3.4 Festivals: Heartbeat of the Year – covers various Jewish festivals from the point of view of Jewish families

3.5 Sukkot: A Festival of Joy – focuses on the festival of Sukkot in detail, and the symbols involved

3.6 You Are What You Wear – introduces the religious garments that many Jewish people wear based on the commandments in the Torah

3.7 Celebrating Life Changes: Bar and Bat Mitzvah – introduces how life-stages are marked in Judaism, with a focus on Bar and Bat Mitzvah

Opportunities for assessment
Summative assessments on the *Judaism OxBox Online* include automarked tests, interactive activities, and self-assessment worksheets.

The end-of-chapter assessment task in the *Student Book* provides formative assessment. Supporting materials for the assessment task can be found on the *Judaism OxBox Online*, such as the Assessment Task Presentation and the related worksheets.

There are other opportunities for assessment too. For example, you could use some of the activities or reflection points throughout each *Student Book* unit, or some of the 'Further Suggestions' at the end of this chapter.

Getting ready for this chapter
- If you have the *Judaism OxBox Online,* watch the case study film clips in advance, so that you can prepare and guide students before and during their viewing.

Objectives and outcomes for this chapter

Objectives	Unit	Outcomes
Most students will:		Most students will be able to:
• explain the origins of Shabbat and the ceremonies that are involved • compare the observance of Shabbat in Orthodox and Progressive Jewish Movements • reflect on the value of creating a 'space in time' in their lives.	3.1	• describe, using sacred text, the origin of Shabbat and how it is marked in Judaism • list similarities and differences in Shabbat observance across the Jewish spectrum • debate the value of creating a special time of reflection, rest and spiritual renewal.
• explain and evaluate the significance of Jewish food laws • analyse the impact of kosher eating on Jewish people's sense of community • reflect on the possible impacts of following certain food rules.	3.2	• list some Jewish food laws and say why they are important to some Jewish people • explain how keeping Jewish food rules affects daily life and a sense of belonging • debate the value of keeping Jewish dietary rules.
• explore the importance of synagogues for Jewish people • identify and explain the key features of synagogues • evaluate the communal activities in their own lives.	3.3	• list the ways synagogues are used in the Jewish community • describe the interior of a synagogue and explain key elements • debate the importance of participating in communal activities.
• explain the significance of some Jewish festivals • evaluate the importance of festivals for the Jewish community • reflect on their own experiences of festivals.	3.4	• describe how Jewish historical events are marked in Judaism and why they are important • explain how both home and synagogue have roles in the celebration of Jewish festivals • describe their own experiences of festivals.
• explore the Jewish festival of Sukkot in more detail • analyse the impact of celebrating Sukkot • reflect on the use of symbols in the festival of Sukkot.	3.5	• using key terms, describe the festival of Sukkot • explain the possible effects of celebrating Sukkot, using what you have learnt from the case-study family • give reasons for the use of the symbols of Sukkot.
• examine what the Torah says about rules for day-to-day clothing • learn about the meanings behind Jewish religious garments • reflect on the possible impacts of wearing religious garments in a multicultural society.	3.6	• give examples from Jewish sacred texts about rules for day-to-day clothing • list some Jewish religious garments and explain why they are worn • debate the issues involved in the wearing of religious garments in a multicultural society.
• explain how different life-stages are marked in Judaism • evaluate real experiences of Jewish rituals and celebrations • reflect on their own views about celebrating life-stages.	3.7	• list examples of how different life-cycle events are marked in Judaism • describe different Jewish responses to rites of passage • explain which life event is most important and why.

The unit in brief

This unit introduces Shabbat, including the ceremonies involved. It highlights how Movements in Judaism keep the commandments differently and have a range of interpretations about what counts as work and rest.

Key ideas

- Shabbat is a day free from work
- It recalls how God rested on the seventh day after the creation of the world
- Shabbat begins on Friday evening with candles being lit and blessings being said, and ends on Saturday evening with another ceremony called Havdalah
- There are differences in Orthodox and Progressive interpretations of Shabbat

Skills practised

- Literacy: creating a tag-line to capture the essence of Shabbat for all Movements
- Analysis: analysing and interpreting case study quotations
- Thinking: considering how laws of Shabbat apply to various activities
- Reflection: reflecting on the creation of a special day in each week

Resources

- 3.1 Shabbat Film Clip A: Shuli and Nina Morris talk about how their family observe Shabbat
- 3.1 Shabbat Film Clip B: Shuli and Nina Morris continue to talk about how their family observe Shabbat
- 3.1 Film Worksheet: students assess their understanding of the case study film clips by linking ideas to the *Student Book*
- 3.1 Shabbat Interactive Activity: students sort activities according to whether or not they would be permitted on an Orthodox Shabbat
- 3.1 Lesson Player: a ready-to-go presentation with built-in resources and teacher notes
- 3 Image Gallery: a useful gallery of photos and film stills from the chapter
- 3.1 Self-Assessment Sheet: students evaluate their learning against the lesson objectives

Ideas for starters

1. Use the Starter from the *Student Book*.

2. Students briefly encountered Shabbat as part of Unit 2.5. Ask the class what they can recall about Shabbat and the rules that Jews are expected to follow. Ask whether they can remember any differences between the interpretations of Shabbat rules by the

different Jewish Movements. Explain that in this unit they will find out more about the different interpretations from case study family members from three different Movements.

3. 'Not working makes Shabbat restrictive/special.' Ask students to vote on which side of this statement they fall. Ask volunteers to explain their views.

4. Ask the class what they would do with a different and special day each week.

Activity guidance

Activity 3 in the *Student Book* could be expanded from a series of small-group debates to a whole-class debate, with a spokesperson selected from each group to start the ball rolling.

Ideas for plenaries

1. Use the Reflection from the *Student Book*.

2. Ask students to close their books and record as many facts from the unit as they can.

3. Ask volunteers to write facts about Shabbat on the board. Then conduct a class vote – most interesting, most surprising, most difficult to understand. Address any remaining questions which students may have about this topic.

4. Ask students, in pairs, to list eight leisure activities that would be allowed on Shabbat.

5. Ask students to mind-map, in three minutes, which activities would not be allowed on Shabbat for Orthodox Jews.

6. Ask students whether they think there is more similarity than difference in the ways in which the different Jewish Movements observe Shabbat. Ask volunteers to explain their views.

Further class and homework activities

1. As a homework, ask students to create a cartoon-strip showing what happens from Friday night to Saturday night in observant Jewish families.

2. 3.1 Shabbat Film Clips A and B on the *Judaism Oxbox Online*.

3. 3.1 Film Worksheet on the *Judaism OxBox Online*.

4. 3.1 Shabbat Interactive Activity on the *Judaism OxBox Online*.

5. Further suggestions on page 62 of this book.

3.2 Let's Think Food

The unit in brief

This unit introduces students to Jewish dietary laws (kashrut). The idea of how kosher eating binds Jewish people to their beliefs and community and strengthens their sense of identity is explored. The different attitudes to kashrut in Jewish Movements are highlighted.

Key ideas

- There are particular dietary laws and restrictions involved in eating kosher.
- Kashrut laws impact Jewish identity and community.
- Jewish Movements have different attitudes to kashrut.

Skills practised

- Literacy: preparing a menu for a kosher meal
- Problem solving: considering reasons why it would be hard for an Orthodox Jew to eat in a non-Jewish home
- Reflection: reflecting on the restrictions of having to follow specific food rules

Resources

- 3.2 Food Film Clip: Laurie and Mrs Reznik talk about how they eat and prepare food in their home
- 3.2 Film Worksheet: students assess their understanding of the case study film clip by linking ideas to the *Student Book*
- 3.2 Food Interactive Activity: students link key terms from the unit with their definitions
- 3.2 Lesson Player: a ready-to-go presentation with built-in resources and teacher notes
- 3 Image Gallery: a useful gallery of photos and film stills from the chapter
- 3.2 Self-Assessment Sheet: students evaluate their learning against the lesson objectives

Ideas for starters

1. Use the Starter from the *Student Book*.
2. Ask the class whether any student has to follow particular rules about what they can eat or drink. At this stage it doesn't have to be religious rules – it could be health-related rules

(e.g. if a student is diabetic). The idea is to introduce the concept of restrictions on diet and what effects these might have on a person's lifestyle.

3. Ask students to pair, share and feed back what impacts they think there might be from having to follow particular dietary rules.

Activity guidance

- It would be useful to take this opportunity to make direct comparisons with the food rules of other faiths that students have studied. Some examples of different foods could be brought in to the lesson (or shown in photo form) and students could be asked to say which ones would be forbidden by which faiths and why.

- Activity 5 in the *Student Book* could be expanded from a series of small-group debates to a whole-class debate, with a spokesperson selected from each group to start the ball rolling.

- You could compare Jewish attitudes to food with other faiths. See Unit 5.4 in the *Buddhism Student Book*, Unit 3.5 in the *Islam Student Book* and Units 4.4–4.5 in the *Hinduism Student Book*.

Ideas for plenaries

1. Use the Reflection from the *Student Book*.

2. Ask students how they would make it possible for a traditional Jewish person to eat in their home – taking into account the laws of kashrut.

3. Ask what the saying 'You are what you eat' might mean in the context of Jewish food laws.

4. 'Kosher – hard or easy?' Ask students to vote on which side of this statement they fall. Ask volunteers to explain their views.

Further class and homework activities

1. Ask students to write a persuasive letter to your school governor requesting that the school canteen serves kosher food for Jewish students, explaining what this would involve.

2. 3.2 Food Film Clip on the *Judaism OxBox Online*.

3. 3.2 Film Worksheet on the *Judaism OxBox Online*.

4. 3.2 Food Interactive Activity on the *Judaism OxBox Online*.

5. Further suggestions on page 62 of this book.

The unit in brief

This unit is about the nature of synagogues and Jewish prayer. It explores the different ways in which synagogues are used, including by different Movements. It focuses on the respect and love that Jewish people have for the Torah, and how this is demonstrated in the treatment of the Sefer Torah in synagogues.

Key ideas

- Synagogues are used for prayer and worship
- Synagogues are also community centres
- Synagogues have key features, for example a Holy Ark
- Love and respect are shown in synagogues for the Torah
- There are different attitudes to prayer; the arrangement of the synagogue; and the role of women according to different Jewish Movements

Useful Word

Aron Hakodesh/Holy Ark, chazan, yad

Skills practised

- Literacy: writing an explanation of the Torah aimed at young children
- Thinking: considering the different ways in which Jewish people show their love and respect for the Torah
- Reflection: reflecting on the importance of communal activities

Resources

- 3.3 Synagogue Film Clip: a congregation in a Liberal synagogue worshipping during a Shabbat service
- 3.3 Synagogue Worksheet: Students label images of features found in a synagogue and answer questions on them
- 3.3 Synagogue Features Interactive Activity: students match images from the unit with their explanations
- 3.3 Lesson Player: a ready-to-go presentation with built-in resources and teacher notes
- 3 Image Gallery: a useful gallery of photos and film stills from the chapter
- 3.3 Self-Assessment Sheet: students evaluate their learning against the lesson objectives

Ideas for starters

1. Use the Starter from the *Student Book*.

2. Ask whether members of the class have ever visited a synagogue. If they have, ask them to give their impressions of it to the class. Ask how it appeared the same or different from other religious buildings they might have visited.

3. Show photos of different places of worship to the class (inside and outside views). Then hold a discussion about what they might be, their special features and the reasons for them. Ask students to identify similarities and differences between them.

Activity guidance

Photographs a–d in the *Student Book* are as follows; the Ner Tamid, dressed Torah scrolls, a menorah, a yad.

Ideas for plenaries

1. Use the Reflection from the *Student Book*.

2. Ask students to discuss, in pairs, what prayer is and whether it's necessary.

3. Ask why Jewish people might choose to pray at home as well as in synagogues.

4. Tell students to close their books and write down four different activities that might take place in a synagogue.

5. Ask students to think about what questions they would like to ask a rabbi in order to find out more about synagogues and Jewish services.

Further class and homework activities

1. Ask students to design a twenty-first century synagogue as a class project. Begin by brainstorming in small groups what it would be like, and then feeding back to the whole class. Students should consider what the synagogue must include and what could be introduced that is new. They should also consider the different approaches of the Orthodox and Progressive Movements in their designs. Is it possible to design a synagogue that all Movements could use?

2. If you used Plenary 5 above, and there is a synagogue located in your area, you could ask the rabbi to visit the class and answer their questions in person, or possibly obtain permission to visit the synagogue itself to address students' questions.

3. 3.3 Synagogue Film Clip on the *Judaism OxBox Online*. Encourage students to ask any questions they have about the service.

4. 3.3 Synagogue Worksheet on the *Judaism OxBox Online*.

5. 3.3 Synagogue Features Interactive Activity on the *Judaism OxBox Online*.

6. Further suggestions on page 62 of this book.

The unit in brief

This unit introduces the many Jewish festivals that occur throughout the year. The role of synagogue and home in celebrating these festivals is highlighted. There is a focus on the experiences and perspectives of case study families from different Jewish Movements.

Key ideas

- There are historical, Biblical and seasonal derivations of Jewish festivals
- Home and synagogue have a role in celebrating festivals
- There are rituals, customs, foods and symbols associated with different festivals
- There are often different perspectives in different Jewish Movements

Useful Words

Hanukkah, Purim, Rosh Hashanah, Shavuot, Simchat Torah, Sukkot

Skills practised

- Literacy: writing a mini-book for young children about a particular Jewish festival
- Thinking: creating an entire multidisciplinary workshop for young children about a particular Jewish festival
- Research: finding out more about Jewish festivals, including one in-depth
- Reflection: reflecting on the enjoyable nature of festivals

Resources

- 3.4 Festivals Film Clip A: The Morris family talk about their favourite Jewish festivals
- 3.4 Festivals Film Clip B: The Morris family continue to talk about their favourite Jewish festivals
- 3.4 Film Worksheet: students assess their understanding of the case study film clips by linking ideas to the *Student Book*
- 3.4 Festivals Interactive Activity: students decide whether statements about festivals are true or false
- 3.4 Lesson Player: a ready-to-go presentation with built-in resources and teacher notes.
- 3 Image Gallery: a useful gallery of photos and film stills from the chapter
- 3.4 Self-Assessment Sheet: students evaluate their learning against the lesson objectives

Ideas for starters

1. Use the Starter from the *Student Book*.

2. Ask volunteers to write down on the board any words they associate with 'festival'.

3. Ask students to write down the names of as many festivals as they can (from any faith). Feed back as a class and highlight any Jewish festivals that may have been named. Follow this up by asking students what they know about those festivals.

4. The festival of Passover (Pesach) has already been covered in Unit 2.6. Ask students what they can remember about that festival from the work they've already done.

5. Ask students to share, in pairs, their memories of any faith celebrations they may have experienced.

Activity guidance

With Activity 2 in the *Student Book*, it might be better to allocate each Jewish festival to different students, or groups of students, to ensure that all the festivals are researched and a broad range of fact sheets are created. Because these fact sheets will be used for other activities, and for reference in later units, they could all be brought together as a class 'festival fact book'.

Ideas for plenaries

1. Use the Reflection from the *Student Book*.

2. Ask students in pairs to write down the names of as many Jewish festivals as they can, including what time of year they occur.

3. Ask a student volunteer to take the Mastermind 'hot-seat'. They have to answer as many questions as they can – from the rest of the class – about a festival of their choice. Repeat this with other students and different festivals.

4. Ask the class to invent a new Jewish Festival to commemorate more recent history.

Further class and homework activities

1. Show 3.4 Festivals Film Clips A and B on the *Judaism OxBox Online*. Ask students to mind-map their Top Five facts or perspectives about festivals from the Morris family.

2. 3.4 Film Worksheet on the *Judaism OxBox Online*.

3. 3.4 Festivals Interactive Activity on the *Judaism OxBox Online*.

4. Further suggestions on page 62 of this book.

3.5 Sukkot: A Festival of Joy

The unit in brief

This unit focuses on one Jewish festival in greater detail: Sukkot. It draws on, and applies, prior knowledge about Jewish festivals and the importance of the home, with reference to a case study.

Key ideas

- Sukkot is the celebration of a time in Jewish history when the Israelites were living in the wilderness
- Jewish people today construct a sukkah (or temporary 'booth') to symbolize the temporary dwellings of their ancestors
- There is symbolism involved in the creation and meaning of the lulav

Skills practised

- Literacy: writing creatively on the theme of refugees and homeless people
- Thinking: considering the meaning of a quotation
- Reflection: reflecting on the impact of the symbolism used at Sukkot

Resources

- ⌇ 3.5 Audio Clip: a recording of Exodus 16:1–15
- ▤ 3.5 Sukkot Film Clip: Jordan Reznik talks about the festival of Sukkot
- ▤ 3.5 Film Worksheet: students assess their understanding of the case study film clip by linking ideas to the *Student Book*
- ⬉ 3.5 Sukkot Interactive Activity: students link key terms from the unit with their definitions
- ⌂ 3.5 Lesson Player: a ready-to-go presentation with built-in resources and teacher notes
- ▣ 3 Image Gallery: a useful gallery of photos and film stills from the chapter
- ▤ 3.5 Self-Assessment Sheet: students evaluate their learning against the lesson objectives

Ideas for starters

1. Use the Starter from the *Student Book*.
2. Ask the class to write down as many types of temporary 'dwellings' as they can in two minutes.
3. Ask students to share with a partner any experiences they may have had of staying in a 'dwelling' that is not a permanent structure.

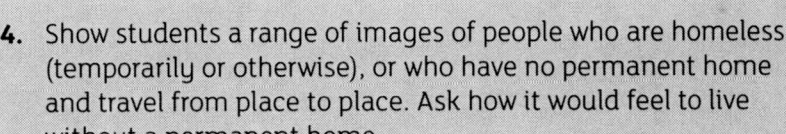

4. Show students a range of images of people who are homeless (temporarily or otherwise), or who have no permanent home and travel from place to place. Ask how it would feel to live without a permanent home.

Activity guidance

Try, if possible, to bring in a lulav to pass around the class to help students understand the construction and symbolism of this important feature of Sukkot.

Ideas for plenaries

1. Use the Reflection from the *Student Book*.

2. Give students one minute to list the names of the Four Species in a lulav.

3. Ask for a student volunteer to answer questions from the class about Sukkot – from the point of view of an observant Jew.

4. Ask students to summarize why Sukkot is important – for example, what is remembered?

5. Ask students to complete the sentence: 'Everyone is entitled to a home because…'

Further class and homework activities

1. As a group activity, you could ask students to design their own sukkah. They should start by writing down the key points from the unit, any important symbols, and the history behind Sukkot. Then, they should research the rules for building a sukkah and what it should include. Students could present their sukkah to the class and explain their decisions.

2. Show Jordan Reznik talking about Sukkot in 3.5 Sukkot Film Clip on the *Judaism OxBox Online*.

3. Play Students 3.5 Audio Clip on the *Judaism OxBox Online*, which is a story from the Torah about the Israelites in the wilderness. Students could generate philosophical questions about the story in a Community of Enquiry.

4. 3.5 Film Worksheet on the *Judaism OxBox Online*.

5. 3.5 Sukkot Interactive Activity on the *Judaism OxBox Online*.

6. Further suggestions on page 62 of this book.

The unit in brief

This unit explores the differences between Jewish religious garments and everyday clothing. The importance of modesty (tzniut) is introduced, as is the idea that Jewish Movements have different attitudes towards clothing. Students are invited to reflect on the significance of what we wear and what it might communicate to others.

Key ideas

- The names of Jewish religious garments, their meanings and when they are worn
- The Jewish concept of modesty in clothing is called tzniut
- There is a difference in attitude to day-to-day clothing between Orthodox and Progressive Jews
- What we value can sometimes be communicated in what we choose to wear

Skills practised

- Literacy: defining and applying two key words: modesty and humility
- Thinking: considering how people show their values through their choice of clothing
- Reflection: reflecting on the possible impacts of wearing religious garments in a multicultural society

Resources

- 3.6 Clothing Worksheet: students identify, describe and analyse four Jewish religious garments
- 3.6 Clothing Interactive Activity: students complete a paragraph about Jewish religious dress
- 3.6 Lesson Player: a ready-to-go presentation with built-in resources and teacher notes
- 3 Image Gallery: a useful gallery of photos and film stills from the chapter
- 3.6 Self-Assessment Sheet: students evaluate their learning against the lesson objectives

Ideas for starters

1. Use the Starter from the *Student Book*.

2. If you can, show real examples of a tallit, tzizit, tefillin, and kippah. Ask students what they could be and why they might be worn.

3. Ask students, in pairs, to talk about what modest dress might mean to them.

4. Show a series of photographs of modern-day dress, including very short skirts, platform shoes, jeans, glamorous dress, casual dress, natural faces, very made-up faces, piercings and tattoos. Ask what the wearers might be trying to communicate.

5. Ask students to discuss in small groups what they think their choice of dress tells others about them. A spokesperson for each group should feed back to the whole class.

Activity guidance

It would be useful to take this opportunity to make direct comparisons with the clothing rules of other faiths that students have studied, particularly the idea of modesty. See Unit 3.6 in the *Islam Student Book*.

Ideas for plenaries

1. Use the Reflection from the *Student Book*.

2. On the board, show the class images of Jewish religious garments or items (you could use 3 Image Gallery on the *Judaism OxBox Online*). Can they identify each item? What does each one symbolize?

3. Ask students to give their opinions about the differences in Jewish men and women's clothing, and also the wearing of religious garments.

4. Refer back to the title of the unit and ask students if it is true that 'you are what you wear'. Can they explain why, or why not?

Further class and homework activities

1. As homework, ask students to plan a lesson about Jewish religious garments to teach the class one year below them. Tell them that they should think about the aims, objectives and resources they would need – and also anticipate any questions that they might be asked.

2. Another possible homework would be to ask students, in small groups, to devise a questionnaire and conduct a survey around the school with the title: 'What Do Our Clothes Say About Us?' The findings could be presented next lesson.

3. 3.6 Clothing Worksheet on the *Judaism OxBox Online*.

4. 3.6 Clothing Interactive Activity on the *Judaism OxBox Online*.

5. Further suggestions on page 62 of this book.

The unit in brief

This unit uses case study quotations to introduce those lifecycle events which are significant in Judaism – with an emphasis on the rituals involved in Bar and Bat Mitzvah.

Key ideas

- There are a number of key life cycle events in Judaism
- There are rituals, customs and symbols for these rites of passage
- Bar and Bat Mitzvah is a Jewish rite of passage for young Jewish boys and girls
- There are more religious and community obligations for Jewish people post-Bar/Bat Mitzvah

Useful Words

Bar/Bat Mitzvah, brit milah, daven, Haftarah, huppa, ma'asim tovim

Skills practised

- Literacy: writing a reflection or poem about the impact of Bar/Bat Mitzvah
- Thinking: considering own views about two statements; comparing the attitudes of different Jewish Movements
- Reflection: reflecting on the most important life cycle event

Resources

- 🎞 3.7 Bar/Bat Mitzvah Film Clip A: Jordan and Laurie Reznik talk about Bar and Bat Mitzvah in Orthodox Judaism
- 🎞 3.7 Bar/Bat Mitzvah Film Clip B: Nina and Shuli Morris talk about Bar and Bat Mitzvah in Reform Judaism
- 📄 3.7 Film Worksheet: students assess their understanding of the case study film clips by linking ideas to the *Student Book*
- 🖱 3.7 Bar/Bat Mitzvah Interactive Activity: students select statements that are true about Bar and Bat Mitzvah
- 🎓 3.7 Lesson Player: a ready-to-go presentation with built-in resources and teacher notes
- 🖥 3 Image Gallery: a useful gallery of photos and film stills from the chapter
- 📄 3.7 Self-Assessment Sheet: students evaluate their learning against the lesson objectives

Ideas for starters

1. Use the Starter from the *Student Book*.

2. Ask students to write down as many life cycle events as they can.

3. Ask which life-stage students think Bar and Bat Mitzvah marks and celebrates.

4. Ask students, in pairs, to consider what Jewish young people might be allowed to do in the synagogue and community after they come of age.

5. Ask students whether they can name any other faith ceremonies that mark the transition from childhood into adulthood.

Activity guidance

You could expand on the activity in the *Student Book* comparing how other faiths celebrate or mark the human life cycle. If there is no time during the lesson, students could be asked to make some comparisons for homework, which they can then feed back at the beginning of next lesson.

Ideas for plenaries

1. Use the Reflection from the *Student Book*.

2. Ask students to sum up Bar and Bat Mitzvah in a sentence.

3. Ask for a volunteer to be in the Mastermind hot-seat – answering questions about Bar and Bat Mitzvah. They should answer as if they are Nina or Shuli Morris (from the Reform Jewish Movement). Repeat the activity with a second volunteer answering as if they are Jordan or Laurie Reznik (from the Modern Orthodox Jewish Movement).

4. Ask students to complete this sentence: 'Celebrating lifecycle events is important whether you are religious or not because…' Display and discuss the responses.

Further class and homework activities

1. Ask students to choose a rite of passage from another faith they are studying and compare it to the equivalent in Judaism. For example, how similar is confirmation in Christianity, or Amrit in Sikhism, to Jewish coming-of-age ceremonies? What are the differences?

2. 3.7 Bar/Bat Mitzvah Film Clips A and B on the *Judaism OxBox Online*. Jewish Movements have different approaches to Bar and Bat Mitzvah. Ask students to create a tag-line to encompass what the Movements have in common.

3. 3.7 Film Worksheet on the *Judaism OxBox Online*.

4. 3.7 Bar/Bat Mitzvah Interactive Activity on the *Judaism OxBox Online*.

5. Further suggestions on page 62 of this book.

Chapter 3 Further Suggestions

These suggestions are addressed directly to students.

3.1 Shabbat: A Special Day

1   Research on the Internet with a partner the kabbalistic idea of Shabbat as a 'bride'. Create a five-minute PowerPoint to capture the spiritual essence of the idea. ***

2   Research Shabbat recipes for food that can be made in advance or left cooking overnight. Devise a Shabbat recipe book: Special Foods for a Special Day. Remember the rules of kashrut. *

3   Create a decorative challah cloth with elements of Shabbat using photos, logos, symbols. **

4   Invent a game for young Orthodox children to play on Shabbat which keeps the rules. *

3.2 Let's Think Food

1   Design a hechsher (label to indicate the contents are kosher) to go on food products that are kosher. *

2   Create a 'How To...' pocket-book divided into sections explaining the rules of How To Keep Kosher. *

3   In pairs, research on the Internet. Find four new facts about keeping kosher/kosher food/kosher slaughter of animals. **

4   Take turns to volunteer for the hot-seat! Other students to ask questions about kashrut with the hot-seat student answering as an Orthodox Jew. **

5   How might keeping kosher strengthen the Jewish community? ***

3.3 Synagogues in the Community

1   Research, using the Internet, the steps involved in being called up to read from the Torah in synagogue. Create a PowerPoint presentation giving a step-by-step guide. Keep it visual to help the audience understand. *

2   Devise a brief information booklet for visitors to a synagogue: Dos and Don'ts. It aims to help guide newcomers on what to look out for, expect, and how to behave. *

3   Using the Internet, research different styles of synagogues around the world. What do they have in common and what is different? ***

4   Class Project: With a partner, choose a synagogue either in the UK or abroad. Research its history and the services it offers. Produce a tourists' leaflet about it. Why did you choose the synagogue you did? **

3.4 Festivals: Heartbeat of the Year

1   Write a diary entry recording your experience as a guest at a Jewish festival. **

2   Create a flick-book for a chosen Jewish Festival which gives information about customs, synagogue services, food, symbols. ***

3   Create a Jewish Festivals blog. **

3.5 Sukkot: A Festival of Joy

1   Imagine there is a model sukkah-making competition at your school. Think of an original idea for making a table-top sukkah. Example idea: an edible sukkah made from biscuits/marzipan etc. *

2   Arts and crafts: make a model lulav from fabric/knitting/felt which could be used as a teaching aid for Jewish children. *

3   Design a poster to raise money for a homeless charity such as Centre Point. Explain clearly why having a safe, permanent home matters. ***

3.6 You Are What You Wear

1   Research the principle of shatnez on the Internet. Find out three more facts. *

2   'How To . . .' Devise a simply written step-by step guidebook to 'laying tefillin'. *

3   Using the Internet, research sheitels (wigs). Why do some Orthodox women choose to wear them? **

4   Class Art Project: make a collage of images of religious Jewish garments and day-to-day dress. *

5   In a small group, devise questions to ask an Orthodox Jew and a Progressive Jew about his/her attitude to religious garments and day-to-day dress. **

6   Debate: 'Orthodox Jewish attitudes to day-to-day dress do not apply to the modern world'. ***

3.7 Celebrating Life Changes: Bar and Bat Mitzvah

1   Invent a ceremony or celebration to mark a new rite of passage, for example: leaving primary school and going to secondary school. How might it be marked or celebrated? **

2   Vote for life events. List them and place in order of importance. *

3   Write a dialogue between Nina Morris and Laurie Reznik about their different beliefs about the role of girls in synagogue. ***

4   Create a flyer to go inside a Bar Mitzvah invitation including information that would help a non-Jewish guest to understand what was going on in synagogue and to feel more comfortable. **

5   Devise a persuasive poster aiming to encourage a post-Bar Mitzvah young person to become more involved in synagogue. **

Chapter 3 Assessment

Assessment in the *Student Book*

You will find an assessment task at the end of every chapter which focuses on AT2. In this chapter, the task asks students to write a lively magazine article about three key facts from their Judaism studies.

In the *Student Book* (and on the supporting worksheets), you'll find guidance about levels of assessment that you can use to help your students understand what their work should include. You could ask them to use these criteria for self- or peer- assessment once they've completed the task.

Assessment Task for Chapter 3 (pages **50–51** of the *Judaism Student Book*)

Objectives
- Consider how Jewish people live day-to-day.
- Apply your knowledge about Judaism reflectively.
- Analyse the diversity in religious expression across the range of Jewish Movements.

Task
Choose three of the most significant facts that you have discovered about living day-to-day as a Jew. Write a magazine article explaining these for a target audience of young people who know nothing at all about Judaism. Write in a lively and engaging style.

Assessment in *OxBox Online*

On the *Judaism OxBox Online*, you'll find resources to use when introducing the assessment task to the class.

You can use the *Chapter 3 Assessment Task Presentation* as a front-of-class tool to help your students unpack the assessment criteria, and understand what is expected of them.

Chapter 3 Assessment Worksheets accompany the task, so that once you finish the presentation, your students can easily get started.

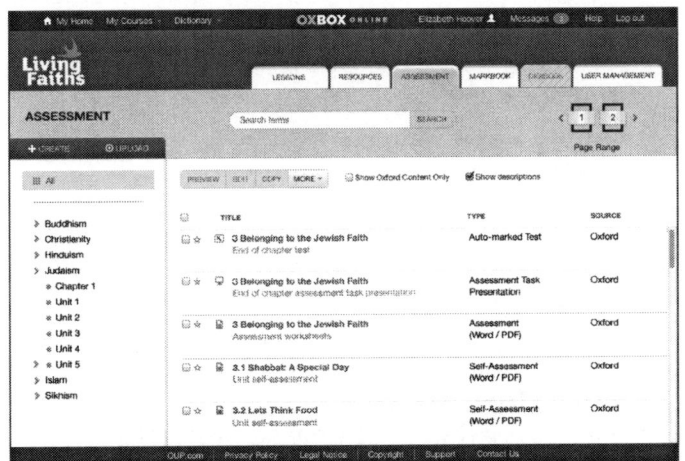

▲ Assessment resources for Chapter 3 on the *Judaism Oxbox Online*

Auto-marked tests

The *Judaism OxBox Online* also contains auto-marked tests for each chapter to help save you time setting questions and marking for AT1. The test for this chapter contains 15 questions and will take most students about half an hour. Test results are automatically stored in the markbook.

Digital markbook

A markbook and a reporting function complete the *OxBox Online* assessment package, so you can keep all your students' test results and assessment scores in one place. This can include the auto-marked tests as well as pieces of work you or the students have marked by hand.

Helping you deliver Key Stage 3 RE

This chapter addresses the following areas of the Programme of Study:

Key concepts

Beliefs, teachings and sources
- Understanding and responding critically to beliefs and attitudes

Meaning, purpose and truth
- Exploring some of the ultimate questions that confront humanity, and responding imaginatively to them

Values and commitments
- Understanding how moral values and a sense of obligation can come from beliefs and experience
- Evaluating their own and others' values in order to make informed, rational and imaginative choices

Key processes

Learning about religion
- Investigate the impact of religious beliefs and teachings on individuals, communities and societies, the reasons for commitment and the causes of diversity
- Evaluate how religious beliefs and teachings inform answers to ultimate questions and ethical issues

Learning from religion
- Reflect on the relationship between beliefs, teachings, world issues and ultimate questions
- Express insights into the significance and value of religion and other world views for human relationships
- Express their own beliefs and ideas, using a variety of forms of expression, including creative forms and reasoned arguments

The big picture

These are the key ideas behind this chapter:

- The value and preservation of human life, and celebrating life, are of central importance in Judaism.
- Rosh Hashanah is a yearly day of judgement.
- There are challenges to practising Judaism in a non-Jewish environment.

- Jewish sacred texts are vague about the afterlife, but the Tanakh refers to Gan Eden, Sheol and Gehinnom.
- The question of evil and suffering is raised when considering events such as the Holocaust.
- Humanity has a responsibility for the environment.

Chapter outline

Use this to give students a mental road-map of the chapter:

4.1 To Life! – explores Judaism's standpoint on human life and its value

4.2 There's No Hiding on the Day of Judgement! – explores yearly times of reflection about behaviour and deeds

4.3 Is Death the End? – introduces Jewish beliefs about death and beyond

4.4 Being Jewish in a Non-Jewish World – considers what it means to be Jewish in Britain today

4.5 Why Do Good People Suffer? – introduces Judaism's arguments about God and suffering

4.6 God's Beautiful World – Who Cares? – examines the Jewish belief in the importance of stewardship of the earth

Opportunities for assessment

Summative assessments on the *Judaism OxBox Online* include automarked tests, interactive activities, and self-assessment worksheets.

The end-of-chapter assessment task in the *Student Book* provides formative assessment. Supporting materials for the assessment task can be found on the *Judaism OxBox Online*, such as the Assessment Task Presentation and the related worksheets.

There are other opportunities for assessment too. For example, you could use some of the activities or reflection points throughout each *Student Book* unit, or some of the 'Further Suggestions' at the end of this chapter.

Getting ready for this chapter

- If you have the *Judaism OxBox Online*, watch the case study film clips in advance, so that you can prepare and guide students before and during their viewing.

Objectives and outcomes for this chapter

Objectives	Unit	Outcomes
Most students will:		Most students will be able to:
• examine Judaism's beliefs about the value of human life and of living well • learn how this belief is expressed by Jewish people • reflect on their own attitude to the value of life.	4.1	• identify, with sacred text examples, Jewish beliefs about the value of human life and living well • describe practices and behaviour that illustrate Jewish value and love of life • debate some issues concerning the value of human life.
• learn about the Jewish belief in an annual Day of Judgement • consider the possible impacts of this belief on Jewish people • reflect on beliefs about judgement and forgiveness.	4.2	• say what you have learnt about the Jewish belief in an annual Day of Judgement and what takes place • describe possible effects of an annual Day of Judgement • explain what they understand by judgement and forgiveness.
• explain Jewish beliefs about death and the afterlife • analyse the impacts of these beliefs on Jewish practices • reflect on their own views about a possible afterlife.	4.3	• identify Jewish beliefs about death and the afterlife • explain some Jewish practices that express these beliefs • debate the existence of an afterlife.
• consider some of the challenges involved in practising Judaism in a non-Jewish society • examine how some Jewish people respond to this issue • reflect on their own views about 'difference'.	4.4	• identify some aspects of Judaism that might be challenging to practise in a non-Jewish society • explain how some Jewish people address this issue • describe their own experiences of 'difference' and state their views.
• identify the difference between natural and man-made evil • evaluate Judaism's arguments about God and suffering • reflect on, and respond to, the effects of the Holocaust.	4.5	• list examples of: 1) natural evil; 2) man-made evil • debate arguments about the suffering of innocent people • state what they have learned about the Holocaust and describe their response.
• examine the Jewish belief in the importance of 'stewardship' of the earth • evaluate the Jewish contribution to environmental awareness • reflect on personal responsibilities towards the environment.	4.6	• define the term 'stewardship' and explain its importance in relation to the environment • give examples of Jewish contributions to environmental awareness • list ways they can show a responsible attitude to their world.

The unit in brief

This unit focuses on the value that Judaism places on human life and the need to preserve it. It also uses case study examples to explore Jewish attitudes to living life to the full.

Key ideas

- Valuing and preserving human life is paramount for Jewish people
- One life is as precious as many
- Judaism emphasizes living this life to the full rather than focusing on the afterlife

Skills practised

- Literacy: writing a journal entry about valuing life
- Thinking: considering how we evaluate Jewish views on harming the body
- Reflection: reflecting on the idea of treasuring and making every day count

Resources

- 4.1 To Life Film Clip A: Hollie and Mrs Walton talk about how they value life in Liberal Judaism

- 4.1 To Life Film Clip B: Laurie and Mrs Reznik talk about how they value life in Orthodox Judaism

- 4.1 Film Worksheet: students assess their understanding of the case study film clip by linking ideas to the *Student Book*

- 4.1 Valuing Life Interactive Activity: students complete a paragraph about Jewish attitudes to valuing life

- 4.1 Lesson Player: a ready-to-go presentation with built-in resources and teacher notes

- 4 Image Gallery: a useful gallery of photos and film stills from the chapter

- 4.1 Self-Assessment Sheet: students evaluate their learning against the lesson objectives

Ideas for starters

1. Use the Starter from the *Student Book*.
2. Ask students what they value most about life. They should write down their key words inside a shape of their choice, for example a heart or a sun.
3. Ask students what they know about birth rituals and celebrations in different faiths. How do different faiths welcome a new human life?

Activity guidance

Activity 2 in the *Student Book* would work well as a whole-class activity. Different students, or groups of students, could choose a particular life cycle event to focus on and then add it to a class collage or wall display.

Ideas for plenaries

1. Use the Reflection from the *Student Book*.

2. Ask a student volunteer to occupy the hot-seat to be asked questions by the rest of the class about Jewish attitudes to valuing, preserving and celebrating life. They should answer from a traditional Jewish standpoint.

3. Ask students to form pairs and devise a dialogue between a Jewish person and a person of no faith about turning off a life-support machine.

4. Ask students to mind-map what they have learned about Jewish attitudes to life.

5. Ask students to create a design for a card to send to a special friend or relative which includes the words 'Treasure Each Day'.

Further class and homework activities

1. What experiences have Jewish people survived during their history? How might such experiences strengthen their desire to live joyfully?

2. 4.1 To Life Film Clips A and B on the *Judaism OxBox Online*.

3. 4.1 Film Worksheet on the *Judaism OxBox Online*.

4. 4.1 Valuing Life Interactive Activity on the *Judaism OxBox Online*.

5. Further suggestions on page 78 of this book.

4.2 There's No Hiding on the Day of Judgement!

The unit in brief

This unit is about the Jewish belief in a yearly Day of Judgement and its effects. It highlights symbolism in the process of repentance and forgiveness.

Key ideas

- Jews believe in an annual Day of Judgement
- The month before the festival of Rosh Hashanah and Yom Kippur is spent in self-reflection
- Jews believe that God is compassionate, just and forgiving of those who repent
- Tashlikh is the symbolic throwing away of sins

Skills practised

- Empathy: considering how a Jewish person might feel about performing Tashlikh
- Thinking: considering good and bad deeds over the past year and how they might be judged
- Reflection: reflecting on the influence of beliefs about judgement and forgiveness

Resources

- 4.2 Tashlikh Worksheet: students reflect on the ritual of Tashlikh in greater detail
- 4.2 Rosh Hashanah Interactive Activity: students complete sentences about the festival of Rosh Hashanah
- 4.2 Lesson Player: a ready-to-go presentation with built-in resources and teacher notes
- 4 Image Gallery: a useful gallery of photos and film stills from the chapter
- 4.2 Self-Assessment Sheet: students evaluate their learning against the lesson objectives

Ideas for starters

1. Use the Starter from the *Student Book*.

2. Ask students to write anonymously on a piece of paper something they are sorry they did, said, or thought. They should screw the paper up and throw it away. Students can feed back on how the process felt.

3. 'Saying sorry is hard/easy'. Ask students to vote on which side of this statement they fall. Ask volunteers to explain their views.

4. Ask whether students have ever found it hard to forgive. Invite them to offer reasons why.

Activity guidance

Follow up Activity 2 in the *Student Book* by holding the debate, either in small groups or as a whole-class.

Ideas for plenaries

1. Use the Reflection from the *Student Book*.

2. Ask students whether they would like an opportunity every year to reflect on their behaviour and possibly seek forgiveness if they are sorry enough. Ask volunteers to explain their views.

3. Symbolically re-create Tashlikh by using a roll of blue paper or fabric to represent flowing water. Ask students to think of something they have done wrong. Give them breadcrumbs to symbolize throwing it away when they are ready. How did they feel? why?

4. Ask students what difference it would make if everyone took some time every year to reflect on the consequences of their actions, or on everything they have done wrong.

Further class and homework activities

1. As homework, ask students to keep a log of a week's behaviour and actions. At the end of the week, they should judge their deeds and behaviour. How did this process make them feel?

2. As another homework idea, ask students to write creatively (using prose, poetry, or dialogue) about the theme: 'Saying Sorry'.

3. Is the belief in judgment about frightening people into being good, or will we be judged? Does it matter which it is?

4. 4.2 Tashlikh Worksheet on the *Judaism OxBox Online*.

5. 4.2 Rosh Hashanah Interactive Activity on the *Judaism OxBox Online*.

6. Further suggestions on page 78 of this book.

4.3 Is Death the End?

The unit in brief

This unit considers Jewish beliefs about life and death. In Judaism, the focus is on living a righteous life, carrying out the commandments of one God. Jewish sacred texts are vague and contradictory about the afterlife, and Judaism places far greater emphasis on what happens now in this life.

Key ideas

- Jewish sacred texts are vague about the afterlife
- The Tanakh refers to: Gan Eden (for the righteous), Sheol (a waiting place while judgement is made) and Gehinnom (for the wicked)
- The emphasis is on life in Judaism
- Jewish burial and mourning practices reflect beliefs

Skills practised

- Literacy: writing a diary entry; writing a response to Jewish ideas about the afterlife
- Research: researching and analysing a famous person's obituary
- Empathy: considering how bereaved Jewish people might feel about the Jewish community's reaction to their loss
- Reflection: reflecting on whether there is life after death

Resources

- ∿ 4.3 Audio Clip: a recording of the Mourner's Prayer
- 📄 4.3 Shiva Worksheet: students conduct research to design a pamphlet on the custom of sitting shiva
- 🖰 4.3 Funeral Rites Interactive Activity: students decide whether statements about Jewish funeral rites are true or false
- 🏠 4.3 Lesson Player: a ready-to-go presentation with built-in resources and teacher notes
- 🖥 4 Image Gallery: a useful gallery of photos and film stills from the chapter
- 📄 4.3 Self-Assessment Sheet: students evaluate their learning against the lesson objectives

Ideas for starters

1. Use the Starter from the *Student Book*. This activity could be attempted as a class 'thumb vote'. You could extend it by asking students to explain which of the following statements they most agree/disagree with and why:
   'When you're dead, you're dead.'

> 'I think some part of us lives after we die.'
> 'I think everyone is judged.'
> 'I think everyone has a soul.'
> 'I think we can live on after we die through the good deeds we have done in our lives.'
>
> **2.** Ask students to discuss with a partner what mourning is, and also consider whether we can mourn other losses – not just death.
>
> **3.** Ask the class for ideas about how a dead person may be honoured and remembered.
>
> **4.** Ask students to write down words that come to mind when they think about the soul.

Activity guidance

- Students' responses to Activity 2 in the *Student Book* would work well as a class mural, particularly if a number of them are visual.

- You could compare Jewish attitudes to life after death with other faiths. See Units 2.5–2.6 in the *Christianity Student Book* and 1.3 in the *Hinduism Student Book*.

Ideas for plenaries

1. Use the Reflection from the *Student Book*.

2. Ask students to close their books and then mind-map what they know about Jewish funerals and mourning practices.

3. Ask students what Jewish sacred texts say about the afterlife, including the names of the possible destinations.

4. 'What is more important – life or the afterlife?' Ask students to vote on which side they come down. Ask volunteers to explain their views.

Further class and homework activities

1. Ask students to take turns telling a partner how they feel about death. As homework, you could ask them to write a written response to sum up their thoughts (perhaps as a poem).

2. Ask students to discuss in pairs or small groups what 'soul' means to them.

3. 4.3 Audio Clip on the *Judaism OxBox Online*.

4. 4.3 Shiva Worksheet on the *Judaism OxBox Online*.

5. 4.3 Funeral Rites Interactive Activity on the *Judaism OxBox Online*.

6. Further suggestions on page 78 of this book.

The unit in brief

This unit draws on, and develops, prior knowledge of Jewish religious practices and customs in order to consider life as a Jew in non-Jewish Britain. It explores the experiences of case study families to focus on what it's like being in a minority group.

Key ideas

- There are challenges to practising Judaism in a non-Jewish environment
- Life as a minority faith group.
- The concept of anti-Semitism.

Useful Words

anti-Semitism

Skills practised

- Literacy: writing a definition of anti-Semitism
- Thinking: creating a role play about a Jewish issue in a non-Jewish society
- Empathy: showing an understanding of the feelings of insiders and outsiders of a group
- Reflection: reflecting on why some people oppose others who are different from them

Resources

- 📽 4.4 Jewish in Britain Film Clip A: Shuli and Mrs Morris talk about what it's like to be Jewish in Britain

- 📽 4.4 Jewish in Britain Film Clip B: Jack and Mr Walton talk about what it's like to be Jewish in Britain

- 📄 4.4 Film Worksheet: students assess their understanding of the case study film clips by linking ideas to the *Student Book*

- 🖱 4.4 Jewish in Britain Interactive Activity: students decide whether statements about living as a Jew in Britain are true or false

- 🎓 4.4 Lesson Player: a ready-to-go presentation with built-in resources and teacher notes

- 🖥 4 Image Gallery: a useful gallery of photos and film stills from the chapter

- 📄 4.4 Self-Assessment Sheet: students evaluate their learning against the lesson objectives

Ideas for starters

1. Use the Starter from the *Student Book*.
2. Ask students to think, pair, share what they already know from their previous studies about Jewish practices and lifestyle in the UK, which demonstrate difference from the majority of people living in Britain, e.g. dietary laws, observing Shabbat, different festivals.

3. Ask students to divide a sheet of paper into two. On one side they should write the heading 'Insider', and on the other side the heading 'Outsider'. They should then add underneath key words to describe their experiences of being both.

4. Ask students, acting as MPs, to devise three new laws to help repair the world (tikkun olam) in terms of the treatment of minority groups. They should firstly discuss in a small group and then choose a spokesperson to feed back to the class.

Activity guidance

When students conduct their research into anti-Semitism for Activity 1 in the *Student Book*, you may wish to supervise closely the websites they access, because some images and information will be disturbing.

Ideas for plenaries

1. Use the Reflection from the *Student Book*.

2. Ask students to complete a spider diagram about the subject of anti-Semitism, with each 'leg' containing words that describe how it makes them feel.

3. Ask students to design a banner or poster with a slogan against anti-Semitism.

4. Ask two volunteers to take the hot-seat and answer questions from the class about keeping the Jewish faith in Britain. One volunteer should answer as an Orthodox Jew and the other as a Liberal Jew.

5. Ask students to close their books and suggest areas of life or Jewish practice that might be difficult for Jews living outside Jewish communities in Britain, e.g. observing the Shabbat.

Further class and homework activities

1. In the speech bubbles Mrs Morris talks about a Jewish tradition of asking questions. Ask students if they can give any examples. You could refer them to Unit 2.6 about the Passover celebrations to encourage their thinking.

2. 4.4 Jewish in Britain Film Clips A and B on the *Judaism OxBox Online*.

3. 4.4 Film Worksheet on the *Judaism OxBox Online*.

4. 4.4 Jewish in Britain Interactive Activity on the *Judaism OxBox Online*.

5. Further suggestions on page 78 of this book.

4.5 Why Do Good People Suffer?

The unit in brief

This unit introduces the question of evil and suffering. It highlights the philosophical debate concerning the existence of evil and suffering in a world created by an all-powerful and all-loving God by focusing on two types of evil – natural and man-made. A case study is used to examine the Jewish response to the Holocaust.

Key ideas

- The presence of evil and suffering in the world
- The classification of evil into natural and man-made
- How evil and suffering can exist with an all-powerful and all-loving God
- The importance of free will and choice
- The existence in human nature of an inclination to the good and the bad (yetzer hatov and yetzer hara)
- Jewish reflections and responses to the Holocaust

Useful Words

genocide, Holocaust, persecution

Skills practised

- Literacy: writing creatively about suffering; creating a pocket book with acts of chesed
- Thinking: considering the impact of persecution on the Jewish people and their views
- Reflection: reflecting on a quotation from a Holocaust victim and what it might say about him

Resources

- 4.5 Holocaust Film Clip: Shuli and Nina Morris talk about how the Holocaust impacts them
- 4.5 Film Worksheet: students assess their understanding of the case study film clip by linking ideas to the *Student Book*
- 4.5 Holocaust Interactive Activity: students complete a paragraph about the Holocaust
- 4.5 Lesson Player: a ready-to-go presentation with built-in resources and teacher notes
- 4 Image Gallery: a useful gallery of photos and film stills from the chapter
- 4.5 Self-Assessment Sheet: students evaluate their learning against the lesson objectives

Ideas for starters

1. Use the Starter from the *Student Book*.

2. Ask students to 'Dare to Share' with the class – to share a time when they felt inclined to do something wrong. Repeat this with an example of the inclination to do good.

3. Ask students to take turns telling a partner how they might turn an evil inclination into an inclination for good.

4. Explain briefly what natural and man-made evils are. Then ask students to play 'Pass the Pebble'. They should pass a pebble around a five-person circle. Invite students to name a natural evil when the pebble reaches them. Repeat for man-made evil.

5. Ask students to think, pair, and share thoughts about why innocent people suffer.

Activity guidance

Activity 4 in the *Student Book* would make a good homework activity. It would also make a creative class project for a presentation to the school on Holocaust Memorial Day.

Ideas for plenaries

1. Use the Reflection from the *Student Book*.

2. Ask students to vote on the following statement: 'Events such as the Holocaust make belief in an all-loving God impossible.' Students could vote with their feet in a continuum, or move to a different part of the room if they agree or disagree.

3. Ask a volunteer to take the 'hot-seat' in the role of God. They should try to answer other students' questions about the existence of evil and suffering.

4. Ask students to write down ways in which the Holocaust can always be remembered, using a mind-map with the word 'Remember!' in the centre.

5. Ask students, in small groups, to devise an event, service, or workshop to remember the Holocaust.

Further class and homework activities

1. As homework, ask students to design a bookmark with a slogan for Holocaust Memorial Day.

2. Show 4.5 Holocaust Film Clip on the *Judaism OxBox Online*.

3. 4.5 Film Worksheet on the *Judaism OxBox Online*.

4. 4.5 Holocaust Interactive Activity on the *Judaism OxBox Online*.

5. Further suggestions on page 78 of this book.

The unit in brief

This unit is concerned with Judaism's beliefs about God entrusting the care of the world to humanity, by introducing the idea of 'stewardship' of the earth and the responsibilities involved.

Key ideas

- The nature and importance of righteous, disciplined and responsible stewardship of the land
- Biblical sources about environmental responsibility
- Human actions and behaviours that influence the environment
- Jewish environmental projects and initiatives which impact the world

Skills practised

- Literacy: writing a persuasive role-play
- Thinking: creating a word cloud about responsible stewardship
- Reflection: reflecting on personal responsibilities towards the environment

Resources

- ⌁ 4.6 Audio Clip: a reading of the Midrash quotation in the *Student Book*
- 📄 4.6 Environment Worksheet: students create a pie-chart which shows the importance of environmental actions
- ⬉ 4.6 Environment Interactive Activity: students complete sentences about Jewish attitudes to care of the environment
- 🎓 4.6 Lesson Player: a ready-to-go presentation with built-in resources and teacher notes
- 🖥 4 Image Gallery: a useful gallery of photos and film stills from the chapter
- 📄 4.6 Self-Assessment Sheet: students evaluate their learning against the lesson objectives

Ideas for starters

1. Use the Starter from the *Student Book*.

2. Ask students what their top five actions showing environmental awareness would be.

3. Ask students how environmental awareness can be shown:
   - at work
   - at home
   - in leisure time .

4. Ask students to vote on whether they think responsible and disciplined stewardship or care of the earth can actually influence the planet.

Activity guidance

- You could ask for volunteer pairings to act out the role-plays they created in response to Activity 3 in the *Student Book*. The class could then vote on the most persuasive or convincing arguments.

- You could compare Jewish attitudes to caring for the environment with other faiths. See Units 4.6–4.7 in the *Hinduism Student Book*, Unit 4.2 in the *Sikhism Student Book* and Unit 5.4 in the *Christianity Student Book*.

Ideas for plenaries

1. Use the Reflection from the *Student Book*.

2. Ask students to summarize 'stewardship' in one sentence, then compare and discuss with a partner.

3. Ask the class what the recipe is for saving the planet – what ingredients are needed?

4. Ask students to write down as many environmentally-aware actions as they can in two minutes.

5. 'Natural resources: live for now or the future?' Ask students to vote on which side of this question they fall. Ask volunteers to explain their views.

Further class and homework activities

1. Collect words and images to create a collage or poster to illustrate the Jewish belief that human beings are responsible for caring for the planet.

2. As homework, ask students to design a cartoon-strip focusing on one environmental issue and how they think Judaism would react to it.

3. Do some research to find out what other faiths, including Humanists, believe about the relationship between humans and the environment.

4. 4.6 Environment Worksheet on the *Judaism OxBox Online*.

5. 4.6 Environment Interactive Activity on the *Judaism OxBox Online*.

6. 4.6 Audio Clip on the *Judaism OxBox Online*.

7. Further suggestions on page 78 of this book.

Chapter 4 Further Suggestions

These suggestions are addressed directly to students.

4.1 To Life!

1   a   Divide up a pie chart into slices for a range of people (choose eight), deciding which lives are more important to save. For example, man of 90, road-sweeper, prime minister etc. How big is each slice? **

    b   Building on what you know about Judaism's attitude to life, what would an Orthodox Jewish person's pie chart look like? Hold a class discussion. ***

2   The Good Life: Carry out a survey to identify the three most important qualities for a 'good' life. Analyse the answers – are they about self or about relationships with others? Discuss your findings as a class. **

4.2 There's no Hiding on the Day of Judgement!

1   In pairs, research Yom Kippur. Create an easy-to-read pamphlet with key elements of the day. *

2   Using the Internet, research Rosh Hashanah customs, food, symbols. Create a five-minute PowerPoint on what you have discovered about the symbolic meaning of these. ***

3   Conduct a survey on the theme of Saying Sorry. Devise questions and collect information. For example: is it enough just to say sorry? What else is involved? Present your findings to the class. **

4   Set up a class vote: Judgement Day or Not? Vote 'yes' if you think a Judgement Day is beneficial and 'no', if not. Write the word on a piece of paper and hold up. *

4.3 Is Death the End?

1   In pairs, conduct a survey on students' beliefs about the afterlife. Make a histogram illustrating your findings. **

2   In the Rabbi's Chair: Interview a rabbi about death and the afterlife. Devise searching questions about everything that confuses you. *

3   Debate: 'There is no such thing as an afterlife. Believing in it just takes away fear of dying'. ***

4   How might a Jewish person answer a child's question on the death of a grandparent: Where has grandpa gone? **

5   'Love is stronger than death'. Discuss. ***

4.4 Being Jewish in a Non-Jewish World

1   Imagine you are starting an email campaign combating anti-Semitism. What would it say? **

2   Create a journal entry for a day in the life of an observant Jewish person focusing on how he/she managed to keep the Mitzvot in a non-Jewish environment. **

3   Debate Abigail Morris's belief: It is good to be part of 'a [minority group]'. ***

4.5 Why Do Good People Suffer?

1   Devise a pie-chart with different sized segments to express what you might do to encourage your inclination to the good (yetzer hatov). *

2   Devise a dialogue that highlights yetzer hara. Repeat for the yetzer hatov. **

3   Research stories of people who suffered in the Holocaust. How do you respond to the stories? How would a Jewish person respond? ***

4   Do some research to find out about the story of Job, a good man who suffered but never lost his trust in God.

4.6 God's Beautiful World – Who Cares?

1   With a partner, take a sheet of A4 paper. Take turns to write a sentence for a collaborative piece of writing about actions and behaviours that are damaging the planet. **

2   In a group of five, stand in a circle and with a softball throw to each other. The person who catches the ball should say a word that might be involved in stewardship of the land. *

3   With a partner, make a list of organizations that aim to care for the environment and its inhabitants. Invent a new one and give it a name. With a partner, devise an informative five-minute PowerPoint presentation about your new environmentally-aware organization. ***

4   'The world has enough for everyone's needs but not everyone's greed' (Mahatma Gandhi). Do you agree with Gandhi? What evidence can you find to support your view? ***

Chapter 4 Assessment

Assessment in the *Student Book*

You will find an assessment task at the end of every chapter which focuses on AT2. In this chapter, the task asks students to write three or four paragraphs about how they think Jewish people would approach the issue of euthanasia, based on their learning so far.

In the *Student Book* (and on the supporting worksheets), you'll find guidance about levels of assessment that you can use to help your students understand what their work should include. You could ask them to use these criteria for self- or peer-assessment once they've completed the task.

Assessment Task for Chapter 4 (pages **64–65** of the *Judaism Student Book*)

Objectives	Task
• Explain, in the light of Jewish faith and practice, how Judaism might respond to a specific issue or dilemma from modern society. • Reflect on your own response to the same issue.	Based on what you have learned in this chapter, how do you think Jewish people might respond to the issue of voluntary euthanasia? Write three or four paragraphs. The specific question you have to answer for this task is: 'Euthanasia goes against Jewish belief. As an Orthodox Jew, do you agree?'

Assessment in *OxBox Online*

On the *Judaism OxBox Online*, you'll find resources to use when introducing the assessment task to the class.

You can use the *Chapter 4 Assessment Task Presentation* as a front-of-class tool to help your students unpack the assessment criteria, and understand what is expected of them.

Chapter 4 Assessment Worksheets accompany the task, so that once you finish the presentation, your students can easily get started.

Auto-marked tests

The *Judaism OxBox Online* also contains auto-marked tests for each chapter to help save you time setting questions and marking for AT1. The test for this chapter contains 15 questions and will take most students about half an hour. Test results are automatically stored in the markbook.

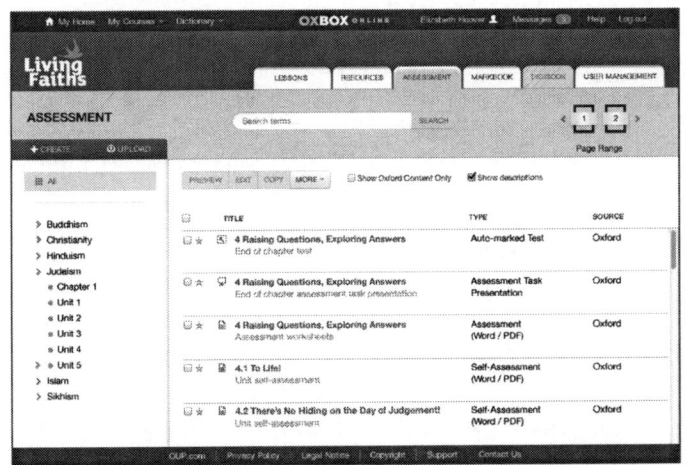

▲ Assessment resources for Chapter 4 on the *Judaism Oxbox Online*

Digital markbook

A markbook and a reporting function complete the *OxBox Online* assessment package, so you can keep all your students' test results and assessment scores in one place. This can include the auto-marked tests as well as pieces of work you or the students have marked by hand.

Helping you deliver Key Stage 3 RE

This chapter addresses the following areas of the Programme of Study:

Key concepts

Practices and ways of life
- Exploring the impact of religions and beliefs on how people live their lives
- Understanding that religious practices are diverse, change over time and are influenced by cultures

Identity, diversity and belonging
- Understanding how individuals develop a sense of identity and belonging through faith or belief
- Exploring the variety, difference and relationships that exist within and between religions, values and beliefs

Key processes

Learning about religion
- Investigate the impact of religious beliefs and teachings on individuals, communities and societies, the reasons for commitment and the causes of diversity
- Evaluate how religious beliefs and teachings inform answers to ultimate questions and ethical issues

Learning from religion
- Reflect on the relationship between beliefs, teachings, world issues and ultimate questions
- Evaluate beliefs, commitments and the impact of religion in the contemporary world
- Express insights into the significance and value of religion and other world views for human relationships

The big picture

These are the key ideas behind this chapter:

- Jewish people believe it is important to transmit the Jewish religion to the next generation.
- There is a biblical commandment to give thanks and give to charity.
- Jewish actions are underpinned by the importance of loving-kindness (chesed).
- The Modern State of Israel is important to Jews today.

Chapter outline

Use this to give students a mental road-map of the chapter:

5.1 Home and Family – covers the significance of home and family in Judaism

5.2 Let's Learn! Teaching the Next Generation – introduces how Jews put into practice the commandment to teach children to love God

5.3 Ancient Religion … Modern Questions … – examines the roles of men and women in Judaism, and questions of sexuality

5.4 Why is Charity Important? – introduces the importance of giving to charity for Jewish people

5.5 The State of Israel: The Promised Land – covers key events in the history of the Jews, including the establishment of modern-day Israel

Opportunities for assessment

Summative assessments on the *Judaism OxBox Online* include automarked tests, interactive activities, and self-assessment worksheets.

The end-of-chapter assessment task in the *Student Book* provides formative assessment. Supporting materials for the assessment task can be found on the *Judaism OxBox Online*, such as the Assessment Task Presentation and the related worksheets.

There are other opportunities for assessment too. For example, you could use some of the activities or reflection points throughout each *Student Book* unit, or some of the 'Further Suggestions' at the end of this chapter.

Getting ready for this chapter

- If you have the *Judaism OxBox Online*, watch the case study film clips in advance, so that you can prepare and guide students before and during their viewing.

Objectives and outcomes for this chapter

Objectives	Unit	Outcomes
Most students will:		Most students will be able to:
• identify and explain faith activities that take place in Jewish homes • evaluate the significance of home and family to Jewish identity • reflect on the influential role of parents and carers in the lives of children.	5.1	• describe some Jewish faith activities that take place in the home • explain the importance of home and family to Jewish identity • state some of the ways families influence children.
• evaluate how Jews put into practice the commandment to teach children to love and worship one God • identify where and how Jewish learning takes place • reflect on their own views about the impact of faith-based schools.	5.2	• give examples of how Jews teach their children to love and worship one God • list different places where Jewish learning might take place • debate the value of faith-based schools in a multicultural society.
• examine the roles of men and women, and questions of sexuality, in modern Judaism • analyse how different Jewish Movements approach these issues • reflect on their own views about the issues raised.	5.3	• explain how modern Judaism has responded to the question of the roles of men and women and sexuality • explain the differences in attitudes to men and women's roles across the Jewish spectrum • debate the issue of equality between the sexes.
• evaluate the meaning of charity (tzedaka) to Jewish people • interpret Jewish sacred texts about charity • reflect on, and respond to, the practice of giving to charity.	5.4	• define the word 'tzedaka' and how Jewish people respond • give examples from Jewish sacred texts about the giving of charity • debate the commandment to give charity.
• learn about events in the history of the Jews, leading to the establishment of modern-day Israel • analyse the importance of the State of Israel to Jewish people • reflect on the issue of Jerusalem's significance to different faiths.	5.5	• list events leading to the establishment of the State of Israel in 1948 • referring to Jewish historical events, explain why the existence of a Jewish homeland might be important to the Jewish people • give reasons for the importance of Jerusalem to different faiths.

5.1 Home and Family

The unit in brief

This unit is about the central importance of home and family in Judaism. It identifies religious practices and celebrations that take place in the home.

Key ideas

- The home is a place of worship, Jewish learning and family celebration
- Jewish occasions are often marked in the home, e.g. Shabbat and festivals
- Several Jewish religious objects and artefacts are found in Jewish homes
- Prayer often takes place at home and sacred texts are used

Skills practised

- Literacy: writing a statement in their own words
- Thinking: considering the implications of a Torah quotation
- Reflection: reflecting on the passing on of information from generation to generation

Resources

- ⎻⋎⎼ 5.1 Audio Clip: a reading of Deuteronomy 6:4–9
- 📄 5.1 Mezuzah Worksheet: students answer questions on the significance of the mezuzah and shema
- 🖱 5.1 Jewish Home Interactive Activity: students link key terms from the unit with their explanations
- 🎓 5.1 Lesson Player: a ready-to-go presentation with built-in resources and teacher notes
- 🖥 5 Image Gallery: a useful gallery of photos and film stills from the chapter
- 📄 5.1 Self-Assessment Sheet: students evaluate their learning against the lesson objectives

Ideas for starters

1. Use the Starter from the *Student Book*.
2. Invite volunteers to write on the board any faith practices (from any faith) that they know happen at home.
3. Ask for volunteers to share any special memories of home celebrations.
4. Ask students what home and family mean to them.

Activity guidance

- If you have access to a mezuzah, it would be useful to show it to the students before they undertake Activity 4 in the *Student Book*.

- You could ask for volunteer pairings to share their discussions in response to Activity 3 in the *Student Book*. The class could then add to their ideas and generate more questions.

Ideas for plenaries

1. Use the Reflection from the *Student Book*.

2. Ask students what they have learned at home and from their family that they have not learned at school.

3. On a sticky note, ask students to write three words to summarize life in a Jewish home. Compare and discuss as a class.

4. Ask for a volunteer to explain what a mezuzah is and why it's important in the home.

5. There is a saying, 'home is where the heart is'. Ask students to discuss with a partner what they think it means. What does it mean for a Jewish family?

Further class and homework activities

1. Ask students the following questions: What special occasions do you celebrate at home? What special traditions are shared by the people who live there? What special meals have you enjoyed? How did you feel?

2. As a homework, ask students to design a mezuzah for their own homes. What symbols will they choose and why? What words will they write on the scroll inside?

3. 5.1 Mezuzah Worksheet on the *Judaism OxBox Online*.

4. 5.1 Jewish Home Interactive Activity on the *Judaism OxBox Online*.

5. 5.1 Audio Clip on the *Judaism OxBox Online*.

6. Further suggestions on page 92 of this book.

5.2 Let's Learn! Teaching the Next Generation

The unit in brief

This unit highlights Jewish education from the perspective of young Jewish people and their families. Questions are raised about the role of faith schools and their advantages and disadvantages.

Key ideas

- The content and nature of Jewish learning
- The advantages and disadvantages of faith-based schools
- God's commandment to Jewish people to pass on the faith to future generations

Useful Words

Hebrew, Ivrit

Skills practised

- Literacy: writing a school prospectus introduction and a letter from a rabbi presenting two sides of an argument
- Thinking: considering the role of education in reinforcing a faith, and in particular, the effects of faith-based schools
- Reflection: reflecting on the impacts of attending a faith-based school

Resources

- 5.2 Faith-Based Schools Film Clip A: Jordan and Mrs Reznik explain why they would promote faith-based schools for Jewish children

- 5.2 Faith-Based Schools Film Clip B: Rabbi Pete Tobias talks about his opinion of Jewish faith-based schools

- 5.2 Film Worksheet: students assess their understanding of the case study film clips by linking ideas to the *Student Book*

- 5.2 Jewish Education Interactive Activity: students complete a paragraph about Jewish education

- 5.2 Lesson Player: a ready-to-go presentation with built-in resources and teacher notes

- 5 Image Gallery: a useful gallery of photos and film stills from the chapter

- 5.2 Self-Assessment Sheet: students evaluate their learning against the lesson objectives

Ideas for starters

1. Use the Starter from the *Student Book*.

2. Give students two minutes to write down some key words about where young people might learn about faith.

3. Ask students to take turns telling a partner where and who influences their knowledge about faith.

4. Ask volunteers to write on the board any ideas they may have for helping learning to leave sweet memories.

5. Ask what the impact might be of children learning about faith from a young age.

Activity guidance

For the second part of Activity 1 in the Student Book, instead of writing from the perspective of Rabbi Pete, you may wish to ask students to conduct their own research into groups that oppose faith-based schools. For example, the British Humanist Association website outlines the reasons why they are campaigning against them. Please note, Rabbi Pete's views are not shared by all Progressive Jews.

Ideas for plenaries

1. Use the Reflection from the *Student Book*.

2. Ask a volunteer to sit in the hot-seat, as the head teacher of a Jewish faith-based school, to answer questions from the class about education. Another volunteer could take the role of Rabbi Pete, or someone with similar views, and a debate could be generated.

3. Ask students to discuss with a partner why teaching Judaism is important to Jewish people.

4. 'Faith-based schools – a good or bad thing?' Ask students to vote on which side of this question they fall. Ask volunteers to explain their views.

Further class and homework activities

1. As homework, ask students to devise a motto and school crest for a Jewish faith-based school.

2. 5.2 Faith-Based Schools Film Clips A and B on the *Judaism OxBox Online*.

3. 5.2 Film Worksheet on the *Judaism OxBox Online*.

4. 5.2 Jewish Education Interactive Activity on the *Judaism OxBox Online*.

5. Further suggestions on page 92 of this book.

5.3 Ancient Religion ...
Modern Questions ...

The unit in brief

This unit addresses issues raised by the practising of an ancient religion in modern society, with a focus on the role of women and sexuality. The views of families from the Reform and Liberal Movements are highlighted and contrasted with traditional thought and practice.

Key ideas

- The concept of egalitarianism is important in Progressive Judaism, in relation to the role of women and of sexuality
- Traditional practices and ideas are sometimes changed or re-interpreted
- There are some issues where ancient and modern are in conflict (for example: roles of men and women, Shabbat observance, gay relationships)

Useful Word

egalitarianism

Skills practised

- Literacy: writing advice as an Agony Aunt or Uncle
- Thinking: preparing arguments for a debate; preparing questions for an interview
- Reflection: reflecting on the sources of advice available to young people

Resources

- 5.3 Role of Women Film Clip A: Shuli and Mrs Morris talk about the role of women in Liberal Judaism
- 5.3 Role of Women Film Clip B: Hollie and Mrs Walton talk about the role of women in Liberal Judaism
- 5.3 Film Worksheet: students assess their understanding of the case study film clips by linking ideas to the *Student Book*
- 5.3 Orthodox and Progressive Interactive Activity: students sort statements depending on whether they apply to Orthodox or Progressive Judaism
- 5.3 Lesson Player: a ready-to-go presentation with built-in resources and teacher notes
- 5 Image Gallery: a useful gallery of photos and film stills from the chapter
- 5.3 Self-Assessment Sheet: students evaluate their learning against the lesson objectives

Ideas for starters

1. Use the Starter from the *Student Book*.

2. Ask students whether they think a religion that began thousands of years ago can still be relevant in a contemporary society with modern issues, such as male and female equality. Ask for volunteers to explain their opinions.

3. Ask the class to discuss, in pairs or small groups, how a Liberal and an Orthodox Jewish person might respond to one of the following modern issues: attitudes to gay relationships, life-support machines, euthanasia.

Activity guidance

• Once students have completed their preparation, conduct a small group or class debate on the statement in Activity 1 of the *Student Book*. If small groups are used, ask a spokesperson for each group to feed back to the class at the end.

• Follow up Activity 2 in the *Student Book* by sharing and comparing advice and then discussing the subject as a class. (References could also be made to how other faiths might address this issue.)

Ideas for plenaries

1. Use the Reflection from the *Student Book*.

2. Oscar Nominations. Ask students to write down the most puzzling, most interesting, and most surprising information they have learned from this Unit. Hold a class vote on the results of the nominations.

3. Follow up Activity 3 in the *Student Book* by role-playing the interview as a summary of the work covered in this Unit.

Further class and homework activities

1. Ask students to research the stories of some significant Jewish women, for example Sarah, Deborah or Esther in the Torah, Rosalind Franklin, Rosa Luxemburg, Anne Frank, or Barbara Streisand. Students should choose one and prepare a short presentation about her life.

2. 5.3 Role of Women Film Clips A and B on the *Judaism OxBox Online*.

3. 5.3 Film Worksheet on the *Judaism OxBox Online*.

4. 5.3 Orthodox and Progressive Interactive Activity on the *Judaism OxBox Online*.

5. Further suggestions on page 92 of this book.

5.4 Why is Charity Important?

The unit in brief

This unit examines the commandment to Jewish people to give a percentage of their income to charity. It focuses on the word tzedaka, which is defined as righteousness.

Key ideas

- There is a commandment (mitzvah) to perform acts of tzedaka
- Tzedaka means righteousness
- A tzedaka box is often kept in Jewish homes
- There is a traditional charitable appeal on High Holy Days
- Friday, before Shabbat, is a traditional time to give tzedaka
- Giving charity is a part of tikkun olam (repairing the world)

Skills practised

- Literacy: creating an advertisement; devising a slogan
- Thinking: considering the meaning of a statement/quotation
- Reflection: reflecting on the role of charity in repairing the world

Resources

- 5.4 Audio Clip: a recording of Leviticus 19:9
- 5.4 Charity Film Clip A: Jack Walton talks about the importance of supporting charity
- 5.4 Charity Film Clip B: Shifra and Mrs Morris talk about why they give to charity
- 5.4 Film Worksheet: students assess their understanding of the case study film clips by linking ideas to the *Student Book*
- 5.4 Charity Interactive Activity: students link key words from the unit with their definitions
- 5.4 Lesson Player: a ready-to-go presentation with built-in resources and teacher notes
- 5 Image Gallery: a useful gallery of photos and film stills from the chapter
- 5.4 Self-Assessment Sheet: students evaluate their learning against the lesson objectives

Ideas for starters

1. Use the Starter from the *Student Book*.
2. Ask students to name three charitable organizations and also explain in one sentence the main work they do.

3. Ask the class, in pairs or small groups, to think about the different reasons that people might have for giving money to charity. Feed back ideas as a class.

4. Ask the class whether there are any ways of being charitable that don't involve money. Ask volunteers to write their ideas on the board.

Activity guidance

- If you have access to a sample tzedaka box, show it to the class before they attempt Activity 1 in the *Student Book*.

- You could take the opportunity presented by this lesson to discuss the topic of charitable giving in other faiths. For instance, one of the Five Pillars of Islam is to give 2.5% of their wealth every year. See Unit 3.2 in the *Islam Student Book*.

Ideas for plenaries

1. Use the Reflection from the *Student Book*.

2. '10% is too much/too little of a person's income to give to charity.' Ask students to vote on which side of this statement they fall. Ask volunteers to explain their views and suggest an alternative percentage.

3. Tell students to close their books and then ask them to list five facts about tzedaka, including the percentage of Jewish incomes that should be given to tzedaka.

4. Ask students to devise a motto to write on a tzedaka box to encourage generous giving.

Further class and homework activities

1. For homework, ask students to design a symbol which represents tzedaka, or to complete Activity 1 in the *Student Book*.

2. Another possible homework would be to ask students to write the speech given by a member of the synagogue for the High Holy Day Appeal to persuade the congregation to give generously to two charities (students can decide which these should be).

3. 5.4 Charity Film Clips A and B on the *Judaism OxBox Online*.

4. 5.4 Audio Clip on the *Judaism OxBox Online*.

5. 5.4 Film Worksheet on the *Judaism OxBox Online*.

6. 5.4 Charity Interactive Activity on the *Judaism OxBox Online*.

7. Further suggestions on page 92 of this book.

The unit in brief

This unit examines the historical persecution of the Jewish people, culminating in the Holocaust and the final establishment of the State of Israel in 1948. It introduces the Law of Return and raises questions about the ongoing difficulties between the Jewish and Muslim Arab peoples of the region.

Key ideas

- Revisiting the concept of the Promised Land and the Jewish exile
- The significance of Jewish persecution and the Holocaust to the establishment of a Jewish State
- The Law of Return
- Continuing Arab-Israeli conflict about land in Israel

Skills practised

- Literacy: writing creatively on the subject of homeland
- Thinking: considering the challenges of living in a shared city
- Research: finding out more about the State of Israel; researching the significance of Jerusalem to three faiths
- Reflection: reflecting on the dispute over Jerusalem and what a perfect multi-faith city would be like

Resources

- 5.5 Israel Film Clip: Nina, Shuli and Mrs Morris talk about how they feel about Israel
- 5.5 Film Worksheet: students assess their understanding of the case study film clip by linking ideas to the *Student Book*
- 5.5 Israel Interactive Activity: students complete a paragraph about the State of Israel
- 5.5 Lesson Player: a ready-to-go presentation with built-in resources and teacher notes
- 5 Image Gallery: a useful gallery of photos and film stills from the chapter
- 5.5 Self-Assessment Sheet: students evaluate their learning against the lesson objectives

Ideas for starters

1. Use the Starter from the *Student Book*.

2. Ask students to discuss, in small groups, what they remember from earlier work about God's promise to the Jewish people about a Promised Land.

3. Ask the class, from their previous work, what they think the Jewish people might feel about living in the State of Israel.

4. Ask students how it might be to share with others something promised to them alone as specially chosen.

Activity guidance

Follow up Activity 4 in the Student Book by exploring the different words and what they might mean to the class. Are there any other words that might be relevant to the conflict between Arabs and Jews?

Ideas for plenaries

1. Use the Reflection from the *Student Book*.

2. Tell students to close their books and then write a brief explanation of why the State of Israel was established in 1948.

3. Ask an Israeli! Ask students to write questions addressed to an Israeli citizen about life in Israel today.

4. Ask students to work in pairs or small groups to create a mind-map, drawing on their learning about Judaism so far – starting with the events in the Garden of Eden, including the covenants with God and showing the constant struggle against oppression and injustice that continues in the 21st century. What questions can students raise?

5. Peace Mission: ask students to work together in small groups to suggest ways of solving the difficulties faced by the Jewish and Muslim peoples in Israel today. Present their ideas and discuss them as a class.

Further class and homework activities

1. Do some research to find out why Jerusalem is so important, not only for Jewish people, but also for Christians and Muslims.

2. 5.5 Israel Film Clip on the *Judaism OxBox Online*.

3. 5.5 Film Worksheet on the *Judaism OxBox Online*.

4. 5.5 Israel Interactive Activity on the *Judaism OxBox Online*.

5. Further suggestions on page 92 of this book.

Chapter 5 Further Suggestions

These suggestions are addressed directly to students.

5.1 Home and Family

1   Devise interview questions for a young Jewish person around your age. What else would you like to discover about Judaism at home? *

2   Design a challah cloth (painting or drawing) decorated with symbols of Shabbat. *

3   Using the Internet, research with a partner the ceremony of Havdalah. Devise a PowerPoint presentation for the class. **

4   Make a poster-sized mind-map of everything you can think of that happens in the Jewish home to do with faith. Three main branches: Shabbat, festivals, rites of passage. **

5   Reflections on Home: Write creatively (prose, poetry, dialogue) about feelings towards home and family including some significant memories. ***

5.2 Let's Learn! Teaching the Next Generation

1   Devise a role-play between two young Jewish people. One attends a Jewish school and one a non-faith-based school. Focus on their experiences of what is positive and negative. **

2   Create a timetable for Year 7 in a Jewish School. Include Jewish Studies, Biblical Hebrew and Ivrit as well as secular subjects. *

3   Devise interview questions for an older person who did not attend a Jewish school to find out how and where he/she learnt Hebrew and Jewish Studies. **

5.3 The Role of Jewish Women in the Modern World

1   Take advertising space on a hoarding in a Jewish area persuading readers to come to a new Liberal Synagogue. Focus on how it makes Judaism relevant to the modern world. **

2   Write a speech defending the Orthodox position on modern issues. ***

3   Devise a tag-line for combining ancient with modern in Judaism. *

5.4 Why is Charity Important?

1   Role-play between one who gives and one who receives tzedakah. *

2   Research mitzvot about tzedakah. **

3   Exit Pass: Record key facts you have learned in today's lesson in a flick-book. Use at the start of next lesson to recap learning and progress. *

4   Charitable giving is a way of putting religious and spiritual ideals into action. How does the Jewish attitude to charity contribute to their belief in healing the world? **

5.5 The State of Israel: The Promised Land

1   Radio Live! Devise interview questions for an Arab and a Jew living in Israel. Aim to discover their attitudes to Israel. *

2   Best and Worst! Devise questions to ask a UK Jewish teenager about five best and five worst aspects about Israel. **

3   Create a friendship bracelet with a message for peace between Arabs and Israelis. *

4   Design a cartoon to explain simply to younger children the story of the establishment of the State of Israel. **

5   Write an account or a poem about what your homeland means to you. **

6   Using your own research, map the journey to the Promised Land. ***

7   Create definitions for the following pairs of words: identity/community, diversity/respect. How are these concepts relevant to the issues raised in this unit? ***

8   How could the Jewish commitment to 'heal the world' provide a strong starting point for working with members of other faiths to resolve conflicts? ***

Chapter 5 Assessment

Assessment in the *Student Book*

You will find an assessment task at the end of every chapter which focuses on AT2. In this chapter, the task asks students to write an essay on five Jewish beliefs and how Jewish people respond to them.

In the *Student Book* (and on the supporting worksheets), you'll find guidance about levels of assessment that you can use to help your students understand what their work should include. You could ask them to use these criteria for self or peer assessment once they've completed the task.

Living Faiths Assessment

Student Book
- Assessment Task
- Levels Guidance

OxBox Online
- Auto-Marked Test
- Assessment Task Presentation
- Assessment Worksheets

Assessment Task for Chapter 5 (pages **76–77** of the *Judaism Student Book*)

Objectives

- Reflect on how Jewish people might behave in response to their beliefs.
- Explore the actions and way of life adopted by Jews in response to their beliefs.

Task

How do Jewish people behave in response to their beliefs? Write an essay which focuses on five Jewish beliefs. Each belief and corresponding response should be explained and evaluated.

Assessment in *OxBox Online*

On the *Judaism OxBox Online*, you'll find resources to use when introducing the assessment task to the class.

You can use the *Chapter 5 Assessment Task Presentation* as a front-of-class tool to help your students unpack the assessment criteria, and understand what is expected of them.

Chapter 5 Assessment Worksheets accompany the task, so that once you finish the presentation, your students can easily get started.

Auto-marked tests

The *Judaism OxBox Online* also contains auto-marked tests for each chapter to help save you time setting questions and marking for AT1.
The test for this chapter contains 15 questions and will take most students about half an hour. Test results are automatically stored in the markbook.

Digital markbook

A markbook and a reporting function complete the OxBox Online assessment package, so you can keep all your students' test results and assessment scores in one place. This can include the auto-marked tests as well as pieces of work you or the students have marked by hand.

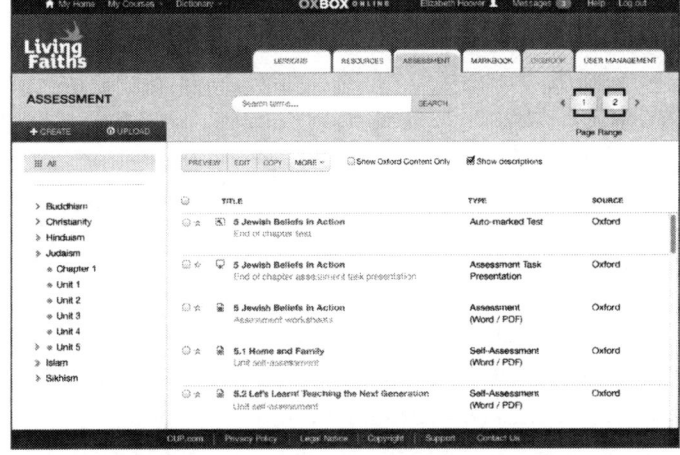

▲ Assessment resources for Chapter 5 on the *Judaism Oxbox Online*

Glossary

Aleinu Key prayer towards the end of each religious service; describes a better world to come

Anti-Semitism Words or actions directed against Jews

Ark/Aron Hakodesh The focal point of a synagogue; a holy cupboard containing Torah scrolls

Bar/Bat Mitzvah Bar Mitzvah is a Jewish boy's coming of age; Bat Mitzvah is a Jewish girl's coming of age at 12 or 13 years old

BCE Before the Common Era, meaning before Year 1 in the Western calendar

Brit milah Circumcision

Canaan Area described in the Hebrew Bible, roughly corresponding to the land of Israel

Chazan Leader of reading, singing and chanting in the services of some synagogues

Chewing the cud The process by ruminants (mammals like cattle, goats and sheep) of regurgitating plant matter from the first stomach to be chewed again

Chief Rabbi The leader of a country's Jewish community; in the UK, the Chief Rabbi is from the Orthodox United Synagogue

Circumcision The removal of the foreskin of male babies (usually at the age of eight days), by a specially trained Jewish person

Covenant Agreement that God would protect the Jews in return for their worshipping Him and following His commandments

Daven Recite prayers

Egalitarianism Equality; often used in reference to the belief in the equal role of women in Progressive Judaism

Exiled Sent away permanently

Genocide The deliberate extermination of a race or group

Haftarah Passages from Nevi'im (Prophets)

Hagadah A book used at the Seder service, telling the story of the exodus

Halakhah Hebrew for 'the way'; Jewish code of conduct affecting every aspect of living

Hanukkah Eight-day winter festival, in which candles are lit each evening; it commemorates the rededication of the Temple in Jerusalem following the Maccabean victory over the Greeks

Hebrew The language of Jewish sacred texts, written from right to left

Holocaust The Nazi government's systematic extermination of six million Jews during the Second World War; often called the Shoah by Jews (meaning 'catastrophe')

Huppah A wedding canopy, symbolizing the marital home

Israelites One of the Biblical names for the Jewish people

Ivrit Modern Hebrew; the language of the State of Israel

Kasher To purge blood from meat by using salt in order to make it kosher

Kashrut Jewish dietary laws and practices

King Solomon Son of King David and builder of the first Temple in Jerusalem; known for his wisdom, power and wealth

Kittel A white robe worn by men in some synagogues during the High Holy Days; also worn by some bridegrooms and used as a burial shroud

Liberal Judaism The most progressive Movement within Judaism

Lulav Palm wand used as part of the Four Species during Sukkot

Ma'asim tovim Good deeds

Megillot Five Scrolls (Song of Songs, Ruth, Lamentations, Ecclesiastes, Esther); contained in Ketuvim, the third section of the Tenakh

Movements in Judaism Groups in the Jewish community that are different from each other in some beliefs, practices and interpretations (for example, Orthodox, Reform and Liberal)

Oral Torah Words that Orthodox Jews believe were spoken by God to Moses, and then written down much later in the Talmud.

Orthodox Keeping to faith rules and traditions in a strict way

Patriarch The father and ruler of a family or tribe, specifically Abraham, Isaac and Jacob

Persecution Harassment, hurt or putting to death, often for religious or political reasons

Progressive Judaism This term includes all Movements within Judaism which have modernized, adapted or reinterpreted Jewish law (e.g. Masorti, Reform, Liberal)

Promised Land The Land of Israel promised to the Jews by God

Prophets Seers or spokespeople transmitting messages from God

Purim A festival commemorating the rescue of Persian Jews; the story is told in the Book of Esther

Rabbi An ordained Jewish teacher; often the religious leader of a synagogue or Jewish community

Reform Judaism One of the Movements within Progressive Judaism which values the traditions but emphasizes flexibility, individual choice and interpretation in living a Jewish life in modern society

Rosh Hashanah The Hebrew words for 'head of the year'; Jewish New Year celebrated in autumn

Ruach Hakodesh Words or messages inspired by God

Sacrifices Offerings to God of wine and grain, or animals; later replaced by prayer

Secular Without religious reference; non-religious

Seder A festive evening service and meal held in the home at Pesach

Shabbat Day commemorating the creation of the world, when God rested on the seventh day; it begins at sunset every Friday and ends at nightfall on Saturday

Shavuot The Hebrew word for 'weeks'; one of the three pilgrim festivals celebrated seven weeks after Pesach (Passover); it commemorates the giving of the Torah

Shema Central Jewish prayer that affirms the belief in one God, and also promotes living a moral life both at home and in the wider world

Simchat Torah An autumn festival celebrating the completion of the year's cycle of Torah reading (celebrated with much joy and dancing with Torah scrolls)

Split hooves Hooves that divide down the middle, e.g. those of a goat or cow

Sukkot A pilgrim festival celebrated in autumn, when temporary dwellings are built to commemorate the Jews wandering homeless in the wilderness

Synagogue Jewish place of worship; also a place of learning and a community centre

Talmud The first writing down of the Oral Torah (Mishnah), and commentary and interpretation of it (Gemara); a guide to Jewish law

Tikkun olam Repairing the world through carrying out mitzvot; it indicates the belief that humanity shares responsibility with its creator

Torah Judaism's central text; comprises the Five Books of Moses (Genesis, Exodus, Leviticus, Numbers and Deuteronomy), and contains Jewish history and laws

Ushpizin The Aramaic word for 'guests'; the tradition of symbolically inviting spiritual ancestors, like Abraham and Isaac, to the sukkah

Written Torah The Five Books of Moses

Yad A pointer, in the shape of a hand, used when reading the Torah

Yom Kippur The Day of Atonement (eighth day after Rosh Hashanah); a solemn fast day when Jews reflect, pray and repent for their wrongdoing during the year

OXFORD
UNIVERSITY PRESS

Great Clarendon Street, Oxford OX2 6DP

Oxford University Press is a department of the University of Oxford.
It furthers the University's objective of excellence in research,
scholarship, and education by publishing worldwide in

Oxford   New York

Auckland   Cape Town   Dar es Salaam   Hong Kong   Karachi
Kuala Lumpur   Madrid   Melbourne   Mexico City   Nairobi
New Delhi   Shanghai   Taipei   Toronto

With offices in

Argentina   Austria   Brazil   Chile   Czech Republic   France   Greece
Guatemala   Hungary   Italy   Japan   Poland   Portugal   Singapore
South Korea   Switzerland   Thailand   Turkey   Ukraine   Vietnam

Oxford is a registered trade mark of Oxford University Press
in the UK and in certain other countries

British Library Cataloguing in Publication Data

Data available

ISBN-13: 978-0-19-838899-9

10 9 8 7 6 5 4 3 2 1

Printed by Bell & Bain Ltd, Glasgow

MIX
Paper from
responsible sources
FSC® C007785
www.fsc.org

Acknowledgements
The publishers would like to thank the following for permissions to use their photographs:

Cover: Godong/Robert Harding/Rex Features; All other photos by OUP

From the author, Sue Schraer: It has been a great privilege to write for this exciting Living
Faiths Series – my grateful thanks to the OUP editorial team. Appreciation also goes to
the following people who assisted both directly and indirectly: Lizzie McWhirter, from RE
Today; Jillian Dunstan, Head Teacher of Mathilda Marks-Kennedy Jewish Primary School;
Pam Goldsmith of the Reform Movement; Rabbi Pete Tobias of The Liberal Synagogue
Elstree; Judi Newman; and most of all, Mike Schraer for his knowledge and constant
support. I am indebted to the three families from across the Jewish religious spectrum who
generously and articulately participated, and shared – with enthusiasm and sincerity –
their experiences, beliefs, and different stances on living life as a Jew in Britain today.

OUP wishes to thank the Reznik, Morris and Walton families for agreeing to take part in
the case study films and to be photographed for this title.

We are grateful for permission to reprint extracts from the following copyright material:

Extracts from The Complete Artscroll Machzor (Mesorah Publications, 1987), reprinted by
permission of the copyright holders, Artscroll/Mesorah Publications, Ltd.

Extracts from the Tanakh: The Holy Scriptures (JPS, 1985), copyright © 1985, 1999 by the
Jewish Publication Society, Philadelphia, reprinted by permission of the University of
Nebraska Press.

Although we have made every effort to trace and contact all copyright holders before
publication this has not been possible in all cases. If notified, the publisher will rectify any
errors or omissions at the earliest opportunity.

The websites recommended in this publication were correct at the time of going to press;
however, websites may have been removed or web addresses changed since that time. OUP
has made every attempt to suggest websites that are reliable and appropriate for students'
use. It is not unknown for unscrupulous individuals to put unsuitable material on websites
that may be accessed by students. Teachers should check all websites before allowing
students to access them. OUP is not responsible for the content of external websites.